STEAM IN MY LENS

THE REGINALD BATTEN COLLECTION
SPECIALLY FEATURING THE GREAT NORTHERN
AND GREAT EASTERN LINES OF THE LNER

STEAM IN MY LENS

THE REGINALD BATTEN COLLECTION
SPECIALLY FEATURING THE GREAT NORTHERN AND GREAT EASTERN LINES OF THE LNER

Malcolm Batten

PEN & SWORD
TRANSPORT

AN IMPRINT OF PEN & SWORD BOOKS LTD.
YORKSHIRE – PHILADELPHIA

First published in Great Britain in 2021 by
Pen and Sword Transport
An imprint of
Pen & Sword Books Ltd.
Yorkshire - Philadelphia

ISBN 978 1 52677 258 9

Typeset by SJmagic DESIGN SERVICES, India.
Printed and bound in India by Replika Press Pvt. Ltd.

Pen & Sword Books Ltd incorporates the imprints of Pen & Sword Books Archaeology, Atlas, Aviation,
Battleground, Discovery, Family History, History, Maritime, Military, Naval, Politics, Railways, Select,
Transport, True Crime, Fiction, Frontline Books, Leo Cooper, Praetorian Press, Seaforth Publishing,
Wharncliffe and White Owl.

For a complete list of Pen & Sword titles please contact

PEN & SWORD BOOKS LIMITED
47 Church Street, Barnsley, South Yorkshire, S70 2AS, England
E-mail: enquiries@pen-and-sword.co.uk
Website: www.pen-and-sword.co.uk

or

PEN AND SWORD BOOKS
1950 Lawrence Rd, Havertown, PA 19083, USA
E-mail: Uspen-and-sword@casematepublishers.com
Website: www.penandswordbooks.com

CONTENTS

INTRODUCTION

Reg Batten was born in 1914, and grew up at Canning Town in the East End of London where an early interest in railways was fired by the sight of Great Eastern Railway tank engines on the Palace Gates to North Woolwich line, along with the numerous freight trains to and from the docks. When he was old enough to visit Stratford on his own, the 'Claud Hamiltons' and B12 4-6-0s further whetted his appetite.

A school visit took him to the British Empire Exhibition at Wembley in 1924 where the LNER Gresley Pacific 4472 *Flying Scotsman* was displayed alongside GWR Castle 4073 *Caerphilly Castle*. He spent so much time in the Hall of Engineering admiring these that he didn't see much else of the exhibition!

He first started taking photographs in 1930, aged 16. The first camera he owned was an Agfa box camera purchased with 100 BDV (Best Dried Virginia?) cigarette coupons. He eagerly loaded this with film and set out to become an ace photographer.

As a railway enthusiast, it was inevitable that trains, especially those of his local LNER, would feature prominently as his subjects! In fact, his first railway shot was of a Gresley Pacific on the heavily loaded 4pm express from King's Cross passing Potters Bar. He followed this with several other railway photographs. Having finished his film, he took it to be processed and eagerly awaited the results. Unfortunately, the results were not all as wonderful as he hoped! He soon found that while pictures of stationary subjects, including trains, were satisfactory, those of moving trains were less than ideal, being somewhat blurred! Like many other newcomers to the photographic hobby, his ambitions exceeded the capabilities of his equipment and his camera did not have a sufficiently fast speed (only 1/30th of a second).

This was replaced by a Coronet folding camera taking 3.5 x 2.5in roll film. Speeds were 1/25th and 1/50th. The lens was good in the centre but tended to vignette in the corners. He soon disposed of this, and it was followed by an Ensign box camera with a wire frame finder. This was a very good, well-made camera, but again limited by a slow shutter speed of 1/30th of a second, which still made it unsuitable for taking trains at speed.

However, by a stroke of luck he managed to overcome this difficulty. He entered a photographic competition, and to his astonishment won first prize, the sum of five guineas – a lot of money in 1934. He purchased a fine second-hand camera, an Ensign roll-film reflex with an Aldis Uno F4.5 lens for the sum of £4 17s 6d. He first tried this out on the LNER, again near Potters Bar, but this time with remarkably more successful results.

In the 1930s the East Coast Main Line (ECML) from Potters Bar tunnel to Brookmans Park was to be a favourite stretch of line, visited on numerous occasions. The other railway companies were not neglected but did not get such extensive coverage. Reg joined the Stephenson Locomotive Society in 1935 and began visiting locomotive depots around London on trips organised by the Society. Generally though, he preferred rural settings to urban locations.

His own railway career was short-lived. He applied for a post in the drawing office at Stratford, where he was taken on trial in 1930. He completed the trial period successfully, and attended technical college, but full-time employment was subject to a medical examination, which to his disappointment he failed. After that he found employment variously as a compositor in the printing trade, working in the photographic trade and latterly in motor insurance.

He didn't only, or even primarily, photograph trains. He always had a love of the countryside and spent many happy days travelling all over the Home Counties and beyond, photographing country scenes and buildings – churches, barns, cottages, old pubs etc. Most of these photographs were taken when either walking or cycling – he and his brother owned a racing tandem on which they covered hundreds of miles. There were far fewer vehicles around in those days, so his photos were generally devoid of such modern incursions as parked cars and yellow road markings, as well as satellite dishes and television aerials.

When war was declared, as a compositor in the printing trade he was classified as being in a 'restricted' occupation at first and so not conscripted, but the rules were changed and he received his call-up papers at the age of

27 in March 1941. His military career started in Wales for he was first drafted to the Royal Army Ordnance Corps (ROAC) at Pembroke Dock. After military training he was then sent to Croydon as a draughtsman. This was ironic, given that he had earlier applied for a post as draughtsman with the LNER at Stratford Works, only to be turned down on medical grounds. Later military experience saw his transfer to the Royal Engineers as an army photographer with a posting at Ripon. This work largely comprised the processing and printing of aerial reconnaissance photographs. After a period at Ripon, he was sent on a course to be trained as an armourer at the RAOC ordnance barracks at Burscough, Lancs. On completing this he was posted to Ruabon in Wales, where he was to spend the rest of the war years. Throughout the war Reg continued to carry a camera wherever he was posted and managed to take some country and railway photos in the more remote locations. Photography in built-up areas, even by someone in military uniform, could arouse unwanted suspicions of spying!

After the war Reg went back to visiting many of his former haunts. In these early post-war years the railways were in a very run-down state. Years of overwork, lack of maintenance and staff shortages had left engines in a filthy condition and often leaking badly. But still they coped! Then came nationalisation, and with it came new numbers and liveries to record. However, after the early part of the 1950s he largely ignored railway photography in favour of other interests.

Many of the country photographs were paying for themselves. He began getting pictures published regularly in such magazines as *Essex Countryside* and the *East Anglian*. He also gained commissions for town guides, calendars and seed catalogues.

Reg was never a prolific railway photographer. In the 1930s black & white still photography was the only real quality option. Although colour film was around, it was too expensive and too slow for general use. Most roll film cameras took either 8, 12, or 16 pictures per spool. Film and processing were both more expensive then, in real terms, than now, so he had to use film sparingly and pick his subjects carefully. Also, the length of the working week gave less time for leisure activities than the present generation receives.

Fares in the 1930s might seem cheap by today's standards but were still dear compared to wage levels

then. There were no discount student, family or senior citizens railcards (not that he would have been eligible for these if there had been). Not being a railwayman, he did not have the advantages of privilege rate tickets. There were early morning workmen's tickets, which he used for travel to work. There were also day and half-day excursion tickets, which he was sometimes able to make use of for photographic trips.

In many ways, photography was easier in steam days. With very little overhead electrification then in place, photographers didn't have to worry about masts and wires in the way. Without the modern culture of vandalism, they didn't have to contend with bridges being meshed in, nor did they have every piece of infrastructure disfigured by graffiti. There was a more relaxed attitude in the days before health & safety legislation. Reg never had a lineside pass, but rarely had any problem photographing from the trackside.

Of course, there were the 'ones that got away'. Reg would ask the ticket inspector at Potters Bar if there was anything special due. On one occasion he was told "Yes, there's the Royal Train, so you had better steer clear of the line." Well he wasn't going to miss this, having come here. He found what he thought was a secluded location by the lineside, sheltering in a sand bin. However, shortly afterwards he felt a tug on his ear. He turned around. It was a policeman.

"What do you think you're doing?" the law asked.

"I'm hoping to take the Royal Train," Reg replied. "Look I haven't got a gun or anything, only a camera."

"Go on, clear off, and none of your cheek," came the reply. So that was that. There were policemen posted on every bridge to ensure a trouble-free journey at a time when the country was moving towards the likelihood of war.

On another occasion he had been out photographing country scenes around the Rye House area of Hertfordshire. He had used all his film and had reached Broxbourne station where he was awaiting a train home. He saw what seemed a strange engine approaching with a motley assortment of coaches. It turned out to be none other than the prototype V4 Class 2-6-2 *Bantam Cock*. He couldn't take it – no film left! He found out later it was working two weeks of trials on the Cambridge line prior to being sent to Scotland. He never saw it again.

In 1965 he realised that BR steam around London would soon be a thing of the past, so spent a few days around Clapham Junction recording the Bulleid Pacifics and BR Standard types that were working out of Waterloo before the impending spread of the third rail.

He was not averse to photographing diesels and electrics on occasion, though rarely setting out to photograph specific classes or workings. Although not included here, after the end of steam he resumed visiting Potters Bar regularly, photographing the 'Deltics' and other classes in both green and blue liveries. When the ECML went the way of the West Coast route and gained the overhead masts, his interest waned however, and he rarely went back thereafter, although he continued photographing diesels and electrics elsewhere around London.

There were still opportunities to take steam though, for now there were the preserved railways and working

museums to visit, such as the Bluebell Railway and Didcot Steam Centre. Later there would be other what we now call heritage railways to visit, the return of main line steam excursions to London and the series of 'Steam on the Met' events from 1989 onwards. With these, a continuing interest in the countryside, and other interests in photographing River Thames shipping and traction engine rallies, Reg continued to be active well into his eighties, until ill health and mobility problems took their toll. Indeed, his final railway photograph was to be of the last train to run on the Stratford–North Woolwich line in December 2006, the very line where his interest in railways was first aroused. Reg died in 2014, aged 100.

Few of these photographs were published in the railway press during the days when they were taken, although he did have the front cover of *Railway Magazine* in May/June 1948 with a picture of Thompson rebuilt A1/1 4470 *Great Northern*. But from the late 1980s onwards, I started writing articles to accompany Reg's photos and submitting them to magazines and heritage railway journals with considerable success. Some of these articles are included in this book. This also led to us making several new acquaintances, and Reg becoming a life member of the Gresley Society.

A wide range of cameras were used over the years, particularly during the period when he was working in the photographic trade and would take different cameras from the shop to try out over a weekend. Negatives range from 3.5 x 2.5in, 2.5 x 2.5in, 35mm etc, while many photos have no surviving negatives. Some were discarded or lost during the war, some deteriorated over the years and some were sold to a commercial company. Until he switched to colour in the 1980s most of his photographs were hand developed and printed in the darkroom he built at home. Reg considered that the skill in getting a good photograph lay as much in the printing as in the composition.

Unfortunately, Reg did not keep accurate records of the date and location of his photographs, and some of the information he did record has become lost over the years. Therefore, many of the dates and some of the locations for these photographs are estimated, as will be noted in the captions.

Malcolm Batten,
London, 2021

FOREWORD

Domiciled in East London from the early 1970s, railway author and photographer **Geoff Silcock** *travelled with his new-found next-street neighbour Reg Batten and Reg's son Malcolm for many years, whilst exploring many of their mutual interests.*

Reg Batten will remain with me a true product of London's East End, and he achieved his finest photographic and literary work from the many journeys, which he saw as adventures, that he undertook for well over six decades. The certain romance of the steam trains that he saw and conjured in print and words is of course headlined in this volume, and these of course include many of the streamlined goliaths constructed under the auspices of *(Sir)* Nigel Gresley to the fore.

And understandably so, as Reg had indeed met and conversed with the great man on more than one occasion, mainly when for several months in 1930 he had worked under the tenure of whom he described as the dour and unpredictable Edward Thompson in the LNER drawing offices at Stratford in East London.

Reg Batten perhaps was never at one with the grimy and, more often than not, fog- and smog-bound East End area from those days, though he did begin to record some of the waterway traffic on the nearby River Thames, including its many turgid backwaters. It was from this time, initially with his younger brother Harry, that they began to take their well-travelled racing tandem bicycle into Essex and sometimes beyond, on their irregular Sundays off, into the 1930s, with Reg composing many photographic images of the village, farming and by-way activities that they came across in their many travels.

Being finally called up in 1941 for military service through the latter part of the Second World War, after his demob Reg would continue his travels into Essex, then mainly by public transport, until the 1960s. By this time he could honestly claim that he had by covered the majority of the county in his photographic quest, and indeed, many of the results of his travels were beginning to grace the magazines of those times, namely as front cover illustrations in the up-market *Essex Countryside* and *East Anglian* publications.

Although Reg Batten and I had known of each other through mutual friends since my move to Manor Park, it took a chance meeting many miles distant to establish that we were indeed next-street neighbours, though both situated at either ends of our adjoining streets, and that many of our interests tallied. Reg was by then in his sixties, and had of course taken many studies of the noble warhorse LNER A4 Pacifics of Nigel Gresley from their inception in the mid-1930s. This was of special interest to me, as I had only photographed these truly iconic locomotives around where I formerly lived at Harringay, at the very end of their reign on the East Coast Main Line from King's Cross to the North.

I was soon to realise that Reg Batten's photographic interests over the years were far more diverse than I could have imagined, and many was the time when motoring into the eastern and southern counties, when seeking out some of the latter-day preserved railway locations contained therein, a distant village church spire might appear on the sky-line, to which he would exclaim "I've already got that!"

And with his such enduring memories, sure enough on my next visit to his green and cream (the colours of his 'native' LNER Tourist Stock 1930s coaches of course) terraced house at the other end from my next-street abode, over tea and biscuits Reg would then regale me with the actual photographic images, and also the circumstances when they were taken.

One episode amongst several *soirées* that stood out from around this time, was when the preserved paddle steamer *Kingswear Castle* ventured upstream from The Pool of London to Putney Bridge. And while it made such laborious progress against the outgoing tidal flow, I was able to let off Reg by several of the riverside bridges *en route*, park the car nearby, and then join him to take our photos. The whole sequence was then repeated in reverse, and we would then set off to our next assignation.

After repeating this several times, it became a point of great hilarity with us, as it did with several camera-clad tourists in the vicinity, who assumed that we must be taking photographs of at least royalty making its way up river. And of course the day's activities were made all the more pleasurable when interspersed with the running commentary from Reg about the former River Thames traffic and wharves in the vicinity, which had given way to a bland modernity since he was young. He also hinted of his former activities as a 'mud-lark' in the proximity.

We also visited several heritage lines in the eastern and southern counties around that time, and this included that of our mutual friend and fellow sage John Jolly at his family Mangapps Farm railway enterprise near Southminster, Essex. Farther afield, in July 2002 there was also the then-embryo Mid-Suffolk Railway at Brockford, where at the time I was involved in photo-chartering the former ex-Great Eastern Railway coaches and wagons there with the visiting M&GN Society's Y14/J15 0-6-0 locomotive No. 564. I found it thought-provoking that the 'The Little Black Goods' itself had been built at our nearby Stratford Works, just two years before Reg Batten had been born locally.

On another trip out of London, we sampled the delights of the Kent & East Sussex Railway from Tenterden, though the latter-day line only ran to Northiam then. This was with one of the Terrier Trust's original ex-London Brighton & South Coast Railway Stroudley 0-6-0Ts at the head of several of the Victorian coaches in traffic there. On the return journey, we had the outside veranda end of the ex-London & North-Western Railway Officers' Saloon all to ourselves, and with the Terrier 'Chaff' flying past overhead, plus the occasional small incendiary char singeing our hair. It all added to the wonderful vintage day out, as did again Reg's commentary describing some of his famed 'expeditions' from East London.

Then although we didn't realise it at the time, came the last trip that the three of us would make together. This was into the heart of the remaining East London docklands itself and was to record the passage of the final passenger train in the area, which was on a rail-tour via Stratford Low Level to North Woolwich in December 2006. Reg was well past his 92nd birthday by then, and was understandably becoming unsteady on his feet, though this didn't dampen his enthusiasm for the day out into what was very much his own home turf.

This event truly marked the end of an era in our East End docks, as we observed the Class 313 EMU edging through what had become a veritable bed of weeds that had proliferated towards the end of normal passenger services, and on towards the 1854 Italianate-style station in the distance. This original station had become the North Woolwich Station Museum from 1984, and an irregular haunt of ours, until that also closed in December of 2008.

Our photographs on that final day were taken from the vantage point of the last former Great Eastern Railway footbridge *in situ* there, which soon afterwards entered preservation itself at the preserved Whitwell & Reepham Station in Norfolk. For well over 120 years it had linked the adjacent Albert Road with the old Tate & Lyle premises in Factory Road by the River Thames across the line to North Woolwich between Silvertown and North Woolwich Stations. This was close to the Royal Docks themselves, and just over two miles as the crow flew from where Reg Batten had spent his formative years in Blake Road, Canning Town, E16, near where nowadays Star Lane Station stands on the Docklands Light Railway.

Despite the slow downward spiral of his health from then on, Reg succeeded in celebrating his hundredth birthday in early 2014, and of course he received the customary letter of congratulation from HM the Queen, which was seen to perk him up no end. As indeed did the personal visit to see Reg arranged by us to mark the event by the then Mayor of Newham Sir Robin Wales, who seemed quite in awe when regaled with just some of Reg's exploits from the distant past, which had evidently included when Gandhi visited the East End in 1931, and the playing of marbles that ensued.

Plus that Reg had been blown off the living room table whilst being bathed where he lived in Canning Town in the 1917 Silvertown explosion, when a local TNT factory had ignited in the neighbourhood, resulting in a great loss of life to local inhabitants. This had affected Reg's overall health and circumstances throughout his long life, for indeed who knows what he might have achieved otherwise. Sadly, Reg passed away a few months later at Newham General Hospital in late December 2014 after a short illness.

Geoff Silcock

ACKNOWLEDGEMENTS/ BIBLIOGRAPHY

ALLAN, Ian, *The A.B.C. of British Railways Locomotives:* (London: Ian Allan, 1958 edition)

ALLAN, Ian, *The A.B.C. of LNER Locomotives* (Staines: Ian Allan, 1943)

ALLEN, Cecil J., *Titled Trains of Great Britain*, 6th edition (Shepperton: Ian Allan, 1983)

GRINDLAY, Jim, *British Railways Steam Locomotives 1948–1968* (Ayr: Modelmaster, 2007)

JACKSON, Joan, *Steam Returns to London* (Shepperton: Ian Allan, 1990)

JONES, Robin, *Steam on the Underground* (Horncastle: Mortons, 2015)

RILEY, R.C., *Great Eastern Album* (London: Ian Allan, 1968)

WHITEHOUSE, Patrick, & THOMAS, David St John, *LNER 150* (Newton Abbot: David & Charles, 1989)

Paintings reproduced by courtesy of Jim Hayes

PRE-WAR DAYS

The Great Eastern Line from Liverpool Street

Although it was his local main line, Reg took few photos on the ex-Great Eastern lines from Liverpool Street. Here LNER B12/3 4-6-0 No. 8558 waits to depart from Liverpool Street Station. The class was introduced by the GER in 1911 with 71 being built. In 1932 the first B12/3 rebuild emerged from Stratford with a larger boiler and round top firebox. It also had a larger superheater and long travel valve gear, while the original decorative wheel valances were removed. Trials showed a saving of up to 20 per cent in coal and water consumption and another 53 were rebuilt to this format by 1944.

LNER B12/2 4-6-0 No. 8573 passing through Stratford with a parcels train. This is one of 10 extra engines built by Beyer, Peacock & Co. in 1928 which never had the valences fitted. It had been intended to order 2-6-4T engines for the Southend line, but following the serious Sevenoaks derailment of a Southern River class 2-6-4T, confidence in this type waned and the order was changed.

Gresley N2 0-6-2T No. 4726 heads into Stratford with a train for Shenfield c.1935. Some of these were tried on the GE section but crews preferred their own familiar N7 class. Not a good quality photo but a rare early one for which no negative survives.

The frames of a pair of ex-GER 2-4-0s (LNER E4 class) Nos. 7441 and 7502 await attention at Stratford works in the early 1930s.

A Trainee Draughtsman at Stratford Works

Stratford became a base for locomotive design and building in 1848, when the Eastern Counties Railway moved its main locomotive workshops from Romford to a site where a repair shop had already been established in 1840. The new works built its first locomotive in 1850 and development was rapid thereafter. By the time the Great Eastern Railway, as it had become in 1862, was absorbed into the LNER in 1923, the works had expanded to cover some 133 acres. This included the wagon building and repair facility at Temple Mills. A world record was achieved in December 1891 when, in response to a challenge, an 0-6-0 goods engine was completed and given a coat of protective grey paint in a time of 9 hours and 47 minutes, a feat never subsequently beaten.

I left school upon reaching my fourteenth birthday in March 1928. I did not initially start work, as my mother had died recently, and my father, who was a skilled boilermaker, was travelling all over the country and said that I would need to stay at home to look after my younger brother and help with the housework. Two years later, I decided that I had had enough of this and wanted to start work.

As a railway enthusiast, you might have expected me to want to become an engine driver. But I knew this was not possible. I wasn't physically strong enough for firing, and since I had needed to wear glasses since age 14, I could not expect to pass the strict eye test.

However, having been top pupil at school in technical drawing, it was not surprising that I decided instead to apply for a post at Stratford Railway Works as a trainee draughtsman in the drawing office.

I was advised to write to a Mr L.P. Parker, who was then in charge. Sometime later I received a reply stating that I was to attend an interview, and at the same time to bring my birth certificate and school testimonial.

The interview was cordial and friendly. Mr Parker was a stern but kindly master. It was decided that I would be granted a trial period in the drawing office as a trainee draughtsman, working under the supervision of the chief draughtsman. I would not be producing original drawings but would be working in the tracing section, where I would also be able to operate the machine which produced blueprints from all the tracings. I was also instructed to take a course in technical drawing at St Mary's College, Bow (now part of the University of London). The Chief Mechanical Engineer, Nigel Gresley, was then one of its patrons.

I was told that I would be working under the direction of Mr Edward Thompson, who on direction from Nigel Gresley was undertaking the rebuilding of the ex-GER B12 class locomotives. I would be introduced to Mr Thompson 'in due course'. This in fact happened a week later, when I was shown into his office by a lady private secretary. He asked me many questions relating to my work at school, my family background and my interest in locomotives. He then stated that if my work was acceptable, and subject to my passing of the strict medical, I would join the permanent staff of the LNER.

Things went very well after the interview and I started on tracings for the B12 rebuilding from slide valves to piston valves. These ex-GER engines had been the mainstay of East Anglian express workings but were now being supplemented by the new Gresley B17 Sandringham 4-6-0s, which had begun to enter service in 1928.

Back in 1930 there were no photocopiers, let alone computers. The original drawings produced by senior draughtsmen would be too valuable to be utilised in the workshops where they might get torn or soiled. So blueprints were produced from tracings made from the original drawings, and it was these expendable blueprints that the workshop staff worked from.

The technique of making blueprints had been known for many years. It was originally devised by Sir John Herschel, and was one of a series of photographic processes he described in a memoir to the Royal Society in 1842. He referred to it as cyanotype. It saw little practical usage at the time, and then lay dormant until 1881, when Marion & Co., photographic publishers, reintroduced it under the name of 'ferro-prussiate or blue process'. They sold the required special coated paper to government departments, engineers, architects, railway companies, shipbuilders etc., wherever there was a need to make reproductions of drawings and plans.

First of all a tracing had to be made. The tracings were made on a translucent linen surface cloth, which was very expensive – I believe at the time it cost around three shillings a yard. This was pinned over the drawing on the board, stretched out taut and fastened by drawing pins. Then a 'pledgit' or ball of cotton wool was dipped in a tray of French chalk and this was applied evenly all over the cloth. The purpose of this was to prepare the cloth so that it would take the Indian ink with which the tracing was executed without causing blots and smudges. The actual tracing was made using the draughtsman's tools of adjustable ruling pens, compasses, dividers etc. Because of the expense of the cloth, mistakes had to be avoided at all costs! In practice I found that small errors could be removed by using a very sharp razor blade gently scraped over the linen.

When a tracing had been completed by a trainee or junior draughtsman, it was initialled and passed to the chief draughtsman. If deemed acceptable, it would be initialled by him, numbered, and dated before being filed away in drawers located below the drawing boards in the drawing office.

When a blueprint was required the relevant tracing was retrieved and taken to a room adjacent to the drawing office. Here, unlike in the well-lit drawing office, the blinds were drawn to give a state of semi-darkness. The blueprints were made on a machine that featured a large cylindrical drum some 40 inches deep. The tracing and a sheet of blueprint paper (some 46ins by 36ins) were wrapped tautly around the inside of this drum. This white paper was sensitised with a mixture of ferric ammonium citrate and potassium ferricyanide. Once the paper was in place, the machine was switched on. The drum encircled a cold cathode lamp. As the machine operated, the drum would rotate and lower in position, exposing the whole of the tracing evenly to the lamp. The light shining through the tracing on to the blueprint paper created the exposure. In the areas of the paper where the light was not obscured by the lines of the drawing, the light reduced the ferric salt to the ferrous state, in which form it reacted with the potassium ferricyanide to form insoluble Prussian blue dye. When the bottom was reached the machine switched off and the blueprint paper was removed. It then had to be washed in a large dish of water to remove the remaining ferric ammonium citrate which had not been exposed, i.e. where the lines of the drawing had prevented this. The paper was then left to dry. The result was a negative in which the lines of the drawing appear in white against a dark blue background - hence the name 'blueprint'. If multiple copies were required the process would be repeated with a new sheet of blueprint paper.

The process was somewhat slow and cumbersome but was the best available at the time. The main snag was if the machine stalled the blueprint would emerge either under- or over-exposed or of uneven density. However, the tracing would be undamaged.

Although my work in the drawing office was considered satisfactory, my career at Stratford was to be short-lived. As Mr Thompson had told me, I was required to undergo a medical examination before I could be taken on as permanent staff. After three months I went for this, and there I failed to meet the medical criteria. This was due to poor eyesight and balance, the result of injuries received in the Silvertown explosion when I was 3 years old. Thus, my employment was terminated and so ended my career on the LNER – though not my interest in railways.

Stratford Works ceased engine building during 1924, having built a total of 1,682 locomotives over a period of a little over 70 years. During this period it also built some 5,500 passenger coaches and over 33,000 goods wagons. However, the works continued to overhaul and repair steam locomotives. This role continued under British Railways. With the displacement of steam by diesels and electrification, part of the works was adapted for diesel locomotive maintenance and repair. Other departments were closed by 1963 and part of the site redeveloped as an international freight terminal. The diesel repair facility was in turn closed in March 1991, bringing to an end a history of railway engineering activity in Stratford stretching back 151 years to 1840.

Taken for a Ride
In 1935, at the age of 21, I started work as a compositor at a printing company near Liverpool Street Station in London and became a member of that long-suffering species – the commuter. I would travel to Liverpool Street direct from my home station at Canning Town on the line from Stratford to North Woolwich, the train using the now-lifted west curve at Stratford that linked the Woolwich line to the main line.

On one occasion though, I boarded the wrong train by mistake. A train had pulled into the station, probably headed by an N7 0-6-2T, and I had boarded it as usual without a second thought, finding an empty compartment. But when the train reached Stratford, instead of turning left as usual, it turned right, to join the main line eastbound by another curve that has also been subsequently removed. "Oh dear!" I thought, "I've got the wrong train, I had better get off at the next station." But the thing was, there were no passenger trains that normally turned right at Stratford. The train didn't stop and just kept on heading eastwards so I had no chance to alight. We passed through Forest Gate, Ilford, and Romford, travelling ever further eastwards and making me later and later for work. As I was alone in my compartment, there was no one to ask where our destination lay. I considered pulling the communication cord, but there were penalties for using this except in emergencies, and I wasn't sure whether getting on a wrong train would be considered an emergency!

Then we reached Shenfield, 18.5 miles from London, which was where my guv'nor lived. As we passed through, I spotted him on the platform waiting for his train – and he saw me! I thought now I would really be in big trouble. Shenfield is where the line to Southend diverges from the main line to Colchester and Norwich. Our train took the curve for the Southend line so at last our destination was clear. The train would have to stop when it reached Southend as this was a terminus.

As we neared the seaside town, I wondered what I was going to say to the ticket collector. Would he believe my story that I had boarded the wrong train by mistake, or would he try to charge me an excess fare – money that I didn't have. But luckily, he did accept my explanation stating, "Well, you've had a bloody good ride for your money hasn't you." "Not really." I replied, "I've probably lost a day's pay over this." However, at last I was able to find out what had happened. The train I had boarded was in fact a private charter – a works staff special outing to Southend from the Tate & Lyle sugar refinery at Silvertown.

The ticket inspector made me out a docket for the journey back to Liverpool Street, and then I was able to make my way back to London, getting to work extremely late, and wondering all the time what sort of trouble I was in. But I needn't have worried – it was all OK when I was eventually able to explain my predicament. We all had a good laugh about it in the print-room – my colleagues demanding to know whether I had brought them any sticks of rock!

The East Coast Main Line from King's Cross in the 1930s

Nigel Gresley introduced his A1 Pacific design for the Great Northern Railway in 1922, and following his appointment as CME of the LNER they became the staple motive power for the East Coast Main Line expresses. No. 4474 *Victor Wild* was built in March 1923. In April–May 1925 this engine was used in comparison trials on the GWR against Castle class No. 4074 *Caldicot Castle*. They worked the 10.30 am Paddington–Plymouth on alternate days, returning with the 12.30 from Plymouth the following day. Similar trials took place on the LNER with No. 4475 *Flying Fox* and GWR 4079 *Pendennis Castle* between King's Cross and Grantham or Doncaster. *Victor Wild* is here seen near Potters Bar in 1937.

A1 No. 2548 *Galtee More*, one of the batch built for the LNER in 1924. This was named after the racehorse that won the 1897 Derby, 2000 Guineas and St Leger races. Taken circa 1936.

A1 No. 2570 *Tranquil* near Potters Bar, circa 1936.

Following the comparison trials with the GWR Castle class, which showed higher coal consumption figures for the LNER engines whether burning Welsh or Yorkshire coal, Gresley made some changes to the design, including fitting long travel valves. From 1927 the A1s were rebuilt with the boiler pressure raised from 180psi to 220psi. The rebuilds became the A3 class (the A2s were the Raven NER Pacifics). New A3s were then constructed from 1928. One of these A3s, No. 2744 *Grand Parade*, is seen working the up Yorkshire Pullman circa 1938. Note the boundary stone on the right.

The predecessors to the Pacifics were the C1 class Ivatt Atlantics. While these started to be displaced from the principal trains, they continued to find work on the main line. No. 3297 is seen hard at work near Potters Bar in 1937.

Another C1 Atlantic, No. 4437 at Potters Bar in 1937. The single lamp on the top bracket indicates that this is a local stopping service.

C1 Atlantic 4403 awaits its next turn of duty at King's Cross 'Top Shed', the photo taken on a Stephenson Locomotive Society visit. On this occasion Reg, along with other visitors, ascended to the top of the coaling tower, whereupon his hat (everybody wore a hat in those days) blew off and was never seen again.

An unidentified Gresley K2 2-6-0 at 'Top Shed' is sandwiched by a pair of N2 0-6-2T locomotives that were the mainstay of the sub-urban services from King's Cross.

The 4-6-0 design was the most popular wheel arrangement for top-link passenger work with British railway companies in the 1920s. The Great Northern Railway had not built any, moving directly from 4-4-2 Atlantics to 4-6-2 Pacifics. By contrast, The Great Central Railway had introduced no less than nine different 4-6-0 classes. Some of these engines were used on the ECML. Robinson mixed traffic B7 class No. 5467 is here on the turntable at 'Top Shed'. These engines gained the unofficial nickname of 'Black Pigs' because of their heavy coal consumption.

Another of the GCR 4-6-0s, B3 6169 *Lord Farringdon*, believed to be on an 'Eason Special' train from Grimsby in July 1937. J.W. Eason was a travel agent in the town who organised these cheap excursions to London from GNR days onwards. The loco was withdrawn in 1948 and the name transferred to A4 No. 60034, previously *Peregrine*. These locos had earlier been used on the 'Harrogate Pullman' on the ECML between 1923–7, but in the 1930s some were based at Immingham.

The Claud Hamilton D16 4-4-0s were a Great Eastern Railway design of 1900 onwards, later much rebuilt. The two "Royal Clauds" 8783 and 8787 were based at King's Lynn for Royal Train duties to Sandringham and were maintained in immaculate condition, with 8783 enhanced with a copper-capped chimney. Royal trains to London used King's Cross rather than Liverpool Street because of the formal protocols needed for royalty entering the City of London. "Royal Claud" 8787 is seen with a train from Cambridge at Welwyn Garden City station in 1938.

In 1935 the nation celebrated the Silver Jubilee of the reign of King George V. The LNER introduced a new high-speed luxury non-stop service between London and Newcastle named appropriately the 'Silver Jubilee', running the 268.3 miles in four hours with one stop at Darlington. To work it, Nigel Gresley introduced his new streamlined Pacific design, the A4 class. Four engines were painted in a silver and grey livery to match the coaching stock and given names with a 'silver' theme. Later, further batches of A4 Pacifics were constructed, many of which were named after breeds of birds. Here, No. 4465 *Guillemot* is on the 'Silver Jubilee'. The location is believed to be near Welwyn Garden City.

In 1937 King George V died and was succeeded by King Edward VIII. However, Edward was to abdicate months later over his desire to marry the American divorcee Wallace Simpson, leading to another coronation as King George VI took the throne. The LNER introduced another luxury non-stop service – the 'Coronation' – between London and Edinburgh which was challenged by their rivals at the LMS with the 'Coronation Scot'. No. 4482 *Golden Eagle* works the 'Coronation' and in this photo is believed to be near Langley troughs by the site of the old Stevenage station.

A4 No. 4498 was built in November 1937 and was named after its designer as it was the 100th LNER Gresley Pacific to be built. Here it works an express passing under Hawkshead Road bridge, Brookmans Park in 1938. Withdrawn in February 1966, this is one of four of the class preserved in the UK.

Another of the A4 Pacifics, No. 4487 *Sea Eagle*, at speed near Potters Bar.

While most local services were in the capable hands of the N2 0-6-2T class, especially those services working through to Moorgate over the 'Widened Lines' where the condensing apparatus came into play, some other trains terminating at King's Cross saw other motive power. This train is headed by Ivatt D2 class 4-4-0 No. 3049, which was to give the photographer an exhilarating and memorable ride.

A Ride to Remember

During the summer of 1936 I decided to spend part of my annual week's holiday at my favourite lineside photographic location – the LNER main line between Hadley Wood station and Hawkshead Road bridge, north of Potters Bar. I travelled up on a local stopper, hauled by the usual N2 0-6-2T, alighting at Potters Bar – a much smaller place then than now! During the day I saw a wide range of Gresley and Ivatt locomotive types from A1 and A3 Pacifics to Ivatt Atlantics and one of the "Royal Claud" 4-4-0s in apple green. K2 and K3 2-6-0s and O2 2-8-0s appeared on freight, while the ubiquitous N2s bustled along on locals. The few new A4 Pacific streamliners, with their distinctive chime whistles, gave you plenty of warning of their imminent arrival.

With film relatively dearer in those days, and only eight or twelve exposures on a roll, I had to be selective about what I photographed. One train that did particularly attract my interest and was duly recorded on film was Ivatt D2 4-4-0 No. 3049 on an up short train of

Gresley coaches which slowed for a stop at Potters Bar. When I later walked back to the station, I enquired of the ticket collector at the barrier for details about this train. He gave me the departure time and stated that it ran non-stop to Finsbury Park, where a stop would be made for tickets to be collected, then on to the 'Cross'.

I decided that I would go back the following day, have a further photographic session, then ride this train back to King's Cross rather than catch the usual slow train back to Broad Street or Moorgate. So I booked a third class cheap day return to Potters Bar, one shilling and eightpence, and off I went. I was back on the up platform in good time – there were only two platforms in those days. I saw her approaching on time and to my delight it was No. 3049 again, the engine I had taken the previous day. I boarded a third-class compartment all to myself. It was a fine one, well upholstered and well sprung. The guard blew his whistle, waved his flag, and we were away. And did we go! The start was electrifying, and from there on No. 3049 went like the clappers. It was as if she were the hare with the hounds snapping at her heels. Stations simply flashed by – Hadley Wood, New Barnet, Oakleigh Park and in no time it seemed we were pulling to a stand in Finsbury Park. It nearly frightened the life out of me, and I had a good mind to alight there and then. But I decided to go on to the 'Cross'. So off we went again after a few minutes and the same cracking pace was maintained. Indeed, we came out of Gasworks Tunnel so fast that I thought we would never stop in time and go right through the buffer stops! When we eventually pulled up, to my relief, the first thing I did was to look at the large clock on the footbridge. We had accomplished the 12.5 miles from Potters Bar to King's Cross with one stop in just 19.5 minutes. Phew! This was an incredible performance for such a small loco. To put

it into context the Class 317 and 365 electric units in the 1990s were allowed 16 minutes for the equivalent journey with a shorter stop at Finsbury Park.

The Ivatt D2 4-4-0 was a class of 70 engines with 6ft 8in wheels, built between 1898 and 1909. Thirty-one of the class passed to BR in 1948, with the last examples being withdrawn in 1951. I do not know where the train I had caught had started from – perhaps Hitchin? But this was probably a regular working for the class at this time. Incidentally there is another photo of the same engine, No. 3049, on a similar train emerging from Hadley Wood tunnel in Patrick Whitehouse and David St John Thomas's book *LNER 150*. The photographer on that occasion was C.R.L. Coles.

In the 1930s the LNER's principal fast freight locomotive was the Gresley K3 2-6-0. With a boiler diameter of 6ft and tractive effort of 30,030lb these capable locomotives had an appearance of strength and power. No. 1583 works a typical mixed fitted freight, probably the famous 3.35 pm London–Edinburgh 'Scotch Goods'. On arrival at Peterborough the London crew would be replaced by a Peterborough (New England) crew for a non-stop run to York. They were allowed a maximum of 55 wagons, a load of up to 650 tons, and a time of 149 minutes for this run of 111.75 miles, at an average speed of 45mph.

Coal was a principal traffic, burned to generate electricity or steam power for industry, to provide fuel for ships and trains, and as a source of heating for most homes. Vast quantities were transported from the coalfields of Yorkshire and the East Midlands, and there was equally a vast quantity of empty wagons to be returned. K3 No. 2450 has charge of a typical rake of these empty wooden-bodied private owner wagons in 1936.

Gresley designed his P1 Class 2-8-2 in 1925 especially for the coal traffic to London. They had a boiler pressure of 180psi and a tractive effort of 38,500lb. Initially they were fitted with boosters increasing their tractive effort to 47,000lb. They were capable of working loaded trains of 100 wagons, perhaps fine on the four-track section of the main line, but beyond the capacity of many goods loops elsewhere. However only two of these impressive locomotives were built and they were both withdrawn in 1945, their boosters having been removed earlier in 1937 (No. 2394) and 1938 (No. 2393). Their boilers were replaced by ones of 220psi in 1942. Perhaps they were a 9F ahead of their time? No. 2393 is seen near Brookman's Park with its booster still fitted.

Also on coal traffic here is N2 0-6-2T No. 4722 on coal emp-ties. Note that this is a non-condensing example.

Coronation Day at Huntingdon

Royal occasions were a cause for widescale celebrations in the East End of London, where I come from. Coronation day, Monday 24 May 1937, when King George VI was crowned, was no exception. Now I wasn't much of a royalist, nor a great partygoer. However, it was a public holiday and thus not to be wasted. This was at a time when annual holidays were only a week off work. There was no 35-hour week and four weeks paid holiday in those days. Modern workers don't know how lucky they are!

I decided to take advantage of a fine day and pursue some photography. I bought a cheap day ticket, price 4s 6d from King's Cross to the old market town of Huntingdon, the birthplace of Oliver Cromwell. I intended to photograph Hinchingbrooke House, once owned by the Cromwell family, and the famous Grammar School, where both Cromwell and Samuel Pepys were educated; along with other fine buildings in Huntingdon and nearby Godmanchester.

I first went to Hinchingbrooke House, and it was here that I met with my first disappointment. It was closed, and lettered 'Private'. I continued to the town and Grammar School, but to my horror found every-where festooned with flags and bunting and quite spoiled for photography. There was a band playing and the locals were feasting and dancing in the streets. In my naivety I hadn't realised that the Coronation would be celebrated in the shires as well as in the capital!

Downcast, I returned to the station. Eating my sand-wiches washed down by a cup of tea in the buffet, I made plans for salvaging the rest of the day with some rail-way photography. I walked northwards up the platform, down the ramp, along the path and under the road bridge till I was abruptly brought to a halt by a voice demand-ing "What the 'ell are you doing here – and what's that box you're holding – are you planning to blow up the railway?" I had underestimated the vigilant lookout of the signalman in Huntingdon North No. 1 signal box. I replied, "I've come up from London to photograph Hinchingbrooke House and the Grammar School, but I've been frustrated by all the flags and bunting in the way." To this he said, "Do you be one of those Roundheads then?" to which I answered, "Not particularly, I'm just interested in history and about Cromwell." "So what are you doing down on the line then?" queried the signal-man. I replied that my main interest was trains, and that I was hoping to salvage something from an otherwise wasted day with some railway photographs. "You won't see many today, there's a special timetable, but provided you don't get on the main line and stay with the gangers I'll turn a blind eye and I'll let you know what's coming." Then he shouted "Eddie!" to the look-out man, "There's another one for you to look after."

I hadn't long to wait before he called from the window that an up express parcels was due at any minute. This duly appeared behind a large-boilered Ivatt Atlantic, No. 4413. Next to come was K2 2-6-0 No. 4654 on a down express. After a gap of about twenty minutes the signalman notified me that a main line express was due, which his colleague had informed him was hauled by No. 4472 *Flying Scotsman*. This was so, and the photograph duly taken. After this had passed I was told that there would be a lull in the proceedings and that if I wanted to stretch my legs I could walk up towards Abbots Ripton where a slow goods train would eventually appear. I took his advice and in due course secured a photo of said goods train, hauled by O2 2-8-0 No. 3488.

Returning to the box the signalman called "Did you get that one?" to which I replied in the affirmative. Then he asked me if I'd like to come up for a 'cuppa' and I gratefully accepted. Then he asked me whether I worked on the railways. "No," I replied, "though I used to. I worked for a while as a trainee draughtsman, down in Stratford Works." "Yes," he replied, "So why didn't you stay? Did you find a better paid job elsewhere?" "No, it wasn't that," I said, "I loved it and wanted to stay on, but I failed the medical and they wouldn't keep me on." "Ah, I'm sorry to hear that," he sympathised.

After a while the bell rang and he appeared to get excited. "Something special?", I queried. "I think you'll like this" he replied, "there's a train coming on the down fast hauled by one of Mr. Gresley's latest V2 class, No. 4774, which is stationed at New England shed, Peterborough. Now if you cross the line, carefully

mind, you can get it coming up." So I thanked him for this news and made my way across the line to await the train. It soon arrived, the new engine polished up, looking quite resplendent in its apple green livery. This splendid sight made my day.

The signalman then asked me what time I intended to leave. "Round about six-thirty," I replied. He checked his working timetable and said "There's a train at 6.45, which stops at Hitchin, Potters Bar, Finsbury Park and the 'Cross'. However, you'll just about get another express in before you go. It will probably be one of the latest streamliners." He was right. When the train did materialise, it was hauled by one of the streamlined A4 class engines, No. 2510 *Quicksilver*.

After I photographed this, my signalman friend stated that he was shortly to be relieved and he wanted me out of the way because his relief was a 'miserable old blighter' who would not look favourably on my lineside presence! But before we parted he slipped me a florin (two shillings) saying "You be sure to send me some of those snaps taken with that big black box, and when you get to the buffet you'll have enough for a cup of tea and a couple of our celebrated Palethorpes' sausage rolls. Those should keep you going until you get home." I thanked him for his kindness, promising to send the photos. These were later duly sent and acknowledged, but I never met him again. When my train arrived, hauled by a K3 2-6-0, I settled down on the cushions as happy as any king on his Coronation day.

Ivatt large-boilered Atlantic No. 4413 on an up express parcels passing Huntingdon North No. 1 signal box. With the ever increasing number of A3 and A4 Pacifics entering service these 4-4-2s were being relegated to such lesser duties.

K2 2-6-0 No. 4654 with a down express passenger train.

The LNER's 'flagship' locomotive – No. 4472 *Flying Scotsman*. Star of a film, and the first British locomotive to be officially logged at 100mph, her exploits were to be somewhat eclipsed in a year's time by *Mallard*'s world record. Note that 4472 was still an A1 at this time and not fitted with a corridor tender.

"...A slow goods train would eventually appear." O2 2-8-0 No. 3488 heads a rake of wooden-bodied coal wagons.

Almost new, and gleaming in spotless apple green livery, V2 No. 4774 passes on the down fast line. Note the three container wagons at the front of the train.

One of the original batch of A4 Pacifics, No. 2510 *Quicksilver*, concluding a satisfactory day's photography at Huntingdon. Built to haul the 'Silver Jubilee', on this occasion it was working a more humble express service.

Stirling Single

The (Number) One That Started it All

Enthusiasts' 'specials' form an important part of the railway scene, and most readers will have fond memories of favourite trips which are readily exchanged whenever they meet. Equally remembered are the 'nightmare' trips when everything seemed to go wrong! The purpose of these excursions might have been to feature specific steam locomotives or diesel and electric classes, or to travel over specific railway lines, perhaps those not usually frequented by such locomotives, or rarely, if at all, by passenger trains.

But how and when did this rich tradition of enthusiasts' railtours begin?

The LNER had been the only one of the big four railway companies to open a public museum to display the historical relics they had accumulated, including a number of locomotives. One of these was the ex-Great Northern Railway, Patrick Stirling designed 4-2-2 No. 1 of 1870. This was the first 4-2-2 design to feature a front bogie. The single driving wheel was of 8ft 1in diameter, boiler pressure was 140psi and the tractive effort was 11,130lbs. Another 37 locos were built up to 1884, but with the grate area increased, followed by ten more from 1884–90 with detail differences. Finally a batch, Nos. 1003–8 appeared in 1894–5, with larger cylinders and grate area, and boiler pressure at 170psi. The single-wheelers were designed to haul trains of 150 tons at average speeds of 51mph between stops. Working alongside Stirling's 2-2-2 engines they achieved fame in the 'Railway Races to the North' of 1888 and 1895. On 21 August 1895, London to Aberdeen was reached in 8hrs 40min at an average overall speed of 60.6mph. Single No. 668 reached Grantham in 101 minutes, at an average speed of 62.7mph, where it was replaced by No. 775, which ran the 82.7 miles on to York in 76 minutes, at an average speed of 65.3mph.

The singles were replaced when heavier trains with bogie coaches were introduced. No. 1 was retired in 1907, having travelled 1,404,663 miles in service. However she was retained for preservation, and later appeared in steam at the Stockton & Darlington Railway centenary parade of 1925 before being placed in the new York museum.

In 1938 the LNER brought the single-wheeler No.1 out of York museum and restored it to working order. This was done with Gresley's approval, who had quite an affection for the veteran. The purpose of this unusual move was for it to work a train of vintage carriages from London to Stevenage as part of a press launch on 30 June for the new rolling stock being introduced on to the 'Flying Scotsman' service. Seven six-wheeled coaches were reconditioned to represent a typical East Coast Joint Stock formation of the 1880s. The single hauled the train to Stevenage, where the invited passengers and press transferred to the modern successor.

No. 1 was later used for a public excursion to Cambridge on 24 August. The single and her vintage stock were booked to leave King's Cross at 11.04am, arriving in Cambridge at 12.46pm. The return journey left at 6.35pm for an arrival time of 8.14pm. The fare was the standard half-day excursion rate of 4s 3d irrespective of class. Some of the passengers chose to travel in Victorian costume for the occasion.

Then the Railway Correspondence & Travel Society, under the inspiration of George R. Grigs, had the imaginative idea of chartering No. 1 and her vintage carriages for a trip to Peterborough for 170 of their members on 11 September 11. As this was on a Sunday and had been announced in advance in the *Railway Magazine* and elsewhere, this enabled many enthusiasts, myself included, to turn out and photograph the veteran. I purchased a cheap day return to St Neots, from where I walked back south to a bridge near Eynesbury. Here I climbed up the bank on to the main line and photographed the special heading northbound out of the mist, with No. 1 proudly bearing the RCTS headboard in front of her chimney.

This was probably the first time that an enthusiasts' society had organised a tour using a specific locomotive, and this pioneering move was to start a trend which has continued to expand ever since.

The RCTS special, seen near St Neots on its way to Peterborough. This photo was recreated as a painting by artist Jim Hayes (*see* frontispiece).

King's Lynn Locoshed 1936

B12/3 No. 8569 awaits its next duty. The turntable at King's Lynn was of 50ft diameter, thus preventing the longer B17s or (in BR days) Britannias from working to here.

Ex-Great Eastern B12s Nos. 8514 and 8530 being oiled up at King's Lynn. In contrast to 8569 both these locos have Belpaire fireboxes and decorative splashers. Both locomotives are fitted with ACFI feed-water heaters on top of their boilers. From 1927 to 1933 a total of 53 locomotives were fitted with the French ACFI system (plus two engines later fitted with equipment transferred from other classmates). This equipment, in the form of large cylinders mounted on the top of the boilers between chimney and dome plus attendant pipework, did nothing for the engine's appearance and gave rise to their nickname of 'Hikers'. The ACFI equipment was removed from 1937, maintenance costs being greater than the fuel and water consumption savings. This photograph was reproduced as a painting by artist Jim Hayes. However, in the painting the 0-6-0T on the right was altered to face chimney first as we thought it would improve the artistic balance!

A front view of B12 No. 8514 showing the ACFI apparatus. There was no mechanical coaling tower at Kings Lynn – coal was shovelled into tubs and thence into the tenders.

An ex-GER D13 4-4-0, No. 8035. Sixty of these engines were rebuilt from 2-4-0s between 1905–8 and from 1913 most gained superheaters. The D13 class did not make it into BR ownership, the last two, Nos. 8023 and 8039, going in 1944.

Ex-GER 0-6-0T No. 7279, LNER class J66. The J66 class was designed by James Holden and built between 1886–9. Of similar dimensions to the later J69 class they had a boiler pressure of 160psi rather than 180psi on the J69s.

One of the stalwart GER J15 0-6-0s, here represented by No. 7520. The design originated under the direction of T.W. Worsdell, who had been appointed as Locomotive Superintendent in January 1882. The first of the Y14 class, as they were known, left Stratford Works in July 1883. The design was a success and eventually 272 would pass to the LNER in 1923. Some withdrawals of locomotives that were only fitted with steam brakes occurred in LNER days, but 127 would pass on to BR in 1948. Their RA1 route availability made them very useful for branch line working.

A Visit to March Locoshed 1937

One day in 1937 I picked up a leaflet relating to a Sunday half-day excursion to Spalding to visit the flower festival held there each year. I noted that the train was routed via March, so I suggested to my friends that if we wrote to the LNER shedmaster at March it might be possible to get a pass to visit the locoshed on the Sunday. To our surprise and pleasure this was duly granted. On arrival we were requested to present ourselves at the gate and then we would be escorted to the shedmaster's office.

So, on arriving at the station we made our way to the shed. We were then told that, as it was a Sunday, there would be nobody available to escort us around the depot. We would, however, be able to roam around at leisure provided that we did not board any locos in steam, interfere with the controls, and we kept away from the coaling stage. We could take photographs, as long as they were not to be submitted for publication without permission from the LNER.

March was primarily a freight shed, newly opened in 1932 to serve the nearby Whitemoor marshalling yards, which were mechanised with humps and retarders at the time. This was one of the largest and busiest marshalling yards in Europe. A large shed, March had an allocation of over 200 locos at the time of nationalisation. Being a Sunday there was a wide variety of locos on shed, representing a good cross section of LNER freight power. There were 0-6-0 types of former Great Eastern, Great Central and Great Northern origins, plus the LNER built J39 class. Larger engines of the K3 2-6-0 and the 02 and 04 2-8-0 types were also to be seen. I was also able to photograph one of the unusual class S1 0-8-4T locos designed by Robinson for the Great Central Railway in 1907. They were originally intended for shunting at Wath marshalling yard, and at the time of their building they were the most powerful engines in Great Britain. Two further examples were built by the LNER in 1932 for use at Whitemoor, and they all lasted until the mid-1950s.

Another engine I photographed was former GER 0-4-4T No. 8123 of class G4. I was told this had just been withdrawn and was one of the last of the class of 40 engines. They had originally been built in 1898–1901 for London suburban work, until displaced by the building of N7 0-6-2Ts.

A GCR 0-6-0 of LNER class J11, No. 5281. One hundred and seventy-four of these engines, designed by Robinson, were built for the GCR between 1901 and 1910. They gained the nickname 'Pom-Poms'.

Robinson GCR class S1 0-8-4T No. 6173. Four of these were built in 1907–8 for heavy yard shunting, with two others added by the LNER in 1932. This was the fourth of the GCR batch. At the time of their building they were the most powerful engines in Great Britain.

Robinson GCR 2-8-0 No. 6257, LNER class 04. First introduced in 1911, these locos were chosen as a wartime standard during the First World War and many were built for the Railway Operating Division. A total of 131 came to the LNER from the GCR, and a further 273 ex-ROD locos were purchased between 1923–7. Many of the class were rebuilt subsequently by Gresley or Thompson. But others remained working in original condition, and one of these, No. 63601, has been retained as part of the National Collection. No. 6257 is one of the ex-ROD locos that were fitted with steam brake only.

A contrast in styles between Gresley 02 class 2-8-0 No. 2956 and the Robinson GCR design.

Gresley O2 2-8-0 No. 2434. The class had been introduced in 1918 for the Great Northern Railway, but this is one of the later LNER built examples with side window cab.

Gresley introduced his J39 class 0-6-0 in 1926 as a standard design. A total of 289 were built but none of these (or of the smaller-wheeled class J38) survived into preservation. No. 1497 is seen here.

Another class J39 0-6-0, No. 2968.

One of Gresley's B17 'Sandringham' 4-6-0s, No. 2821 *Hatfield House*. The class was introduced in 1928 for the Great Eastern section. Some (though not this one) were later rebuilt by Thompson with a '100A' boiler and higher boiler pressure, while others were also modified to two cylinders, becoming class B2. None survived into preservation, although the B17 Steam Locomotive Trust is constructing a 'newbuild' to be named *Spirit of Sandringham*.

Gresley K2 2-6-0 No. 4673. It is noticeable from these photos that not only most of the locomotives are clean, but the trackwork is also clean and tidy with no discarded scrap metal, old oilcans etc. littering the site.

Gresley's larger 2-6-0 design, the K3 class, is represented by No. 2762, a March resident from 1936–8. Note the large water tower behind.

Another K3, No. 2934, leads a line of locomotives outside the shed.

Locomotives of ex-GCR, GNR and GER origin could all be found at March, as well as LNER designs. This is ex-GER J17 0-6-0 No. 8156.

A Holden 0-6-0 of the J19 class, No. 8242 typifies the freight engines inherited from the Great Eastern Railway. This example has been rebuilt from a J18 and is now fitted with a round-topped firebox in place of the original square top design – modifications which took place from 1935 onwards.

A GER veteran! G4 class 0-4-4T No. 8123 (GER class S44). This was based at March from April 1928–August 1938. It was replaced by No. 8139 which was withdrawn from March in December 1938, the last of the class of 40 engines built from 1898–1901. They had originally been built for London suburban work, until displaced by the building of N7 0-6-2Ts. One was used as the March station pilot.

Ex-GER D15 4-4-0 No. 8894 with original style valances. Behind is what appears to be D16 No. 8888, which does not have the safety valve surround fitted to 8894.

LMS Main Lines from London

Until Stanier's arrival the principal express motive power of the LMS was the Royal Scot 4-6-0 class, introduced in 1927. No. 6111 *Royal Fusilier* is at Bourne End in 1937.

The Patriots were effectively a smaller version of the Royal Scots. The first two were nominally rebuilds of LNWR Claughton 4-6-0s. An unidentified pair of Patriots double-head a train at Bourne End near Berkhampstead.

Stanier Jubilee class 4-6-0 No. 5629 *Straits Settlement* on a parcels train at Elstree, c. 1937. The class was introduced by Stanier in 1934 as a taper boiler development of the Patriots.

Stanier introduced his 8F 2-8-0 as a standard design in 1935. 1936-built No. 8032 is on a train of coal wagons, typical of the kind of work these capable engines would perform until the end of BR steam in 1968. Seen at Bourne End in 1937.

Stanier's answer to the LNER A4s was the streamlined Coronation class Pacific. First of the class No. 6220 *Coronation* at Bourne End in 1937 on the 'Coronation Scot'. The stripes on the streamlined casing were extended to the carriages.

No. 6221 *Queen Elizabeth* also seen at Bourne End, in this case on a lesser duty.

Day Trip to Bucks

Knowing my interest in the countryside, a work colleague had been telling me about the village of East Claydon in Buckinghamshire where he had grown up, and the neighbouring villages. Being a keen walker and photographer, one day I decided to go and see some of these places for myself. I discovered that half-day excursion tickets and ramblers' tickets were available at about 4s 6d return. So one Saturday I decided to travel to Bletchley, then catch a train to Winslow on the line through to Oxford. From here I would walk out and cover all the Claydon villages in one day – East Claydon, Botolph Claydon, Middle Claydon, Steeple Claydon and back to Winslow. This I duly did, getting several excellent photographs. I walked back along the railway track for part of the journey – traffic wasn't exactly busy, even in those days. It was while doing this that I took an ex-LNWR Webb 'Cauliflower' 0-6-0 coming along on

a local passenger train. There were 310 of these rather antiquated looking but useful locos built between 1880 and 1902, with all but two coming into LMS stock. I used to wonder how they got the nickname 'Cauliflowers' as there didn't seem to be any obvious derivation. Later someone told me it was because the large LNWR crest on these engines in their pre-LMS days looked a bit like a cauliflower when seen from a distance. Well it suppose it might have after a few pints of the Aylesbury Brewing Company's best!

Arriving back at Winslow, I caught a train back to Bletchley. Still having an exposure left on my film, and with the afternoon still being fine and sunny, I caught a train back to Berkhamstead and then walked to a point near Bourne End that I had frequented before for railway photos. Here I took a picture of a Royal Scot on a down express, thus finishing my film and bringing to an end an enjoyable day's photographic excursion.

At Bletchley the West Coast Main Line is crossed by the line from Cambridge through to Oxford. A veteran LNWR 'Cauliflower' 0-6-0 works a local train along this line near Winslow in 1937. There were 310 of these rather antiquated looking but useful locos built between 1880 and 1902, with all but two coming into LMS stock.

LMS Shed Visits 1937–8

Stanier's 'scrap and build' policy was to see an early end for many of the ex-LNWR passenger locos. Bowen-Cooke LNWR 'Prince of Wales' 4-6-0 No. 25751 receives the attention of the cleaners at Camden. Introduced in 1911, only six of this class (not including this example) were to pass to British Railways, but all had gone by the end of 1949, with none receiving their new BR numbers.

'Royal Scot' No. 6154 *The Hussar* at Camden, cleaned, coaled and ready for its next duty.

William Stanier's first design for the LMS was a Pacific to rival the LNER designs and power trains from London to Glasgow. The result was the 'Princess Royal' class introduced in 1933, also known to railwaymen and enthusiasts as 'Lizzies' This is No. 6206, named *Princess Marie Louise*, on Camden depot.

While Camden was the principal passenger depot for the WCML in London, Willesden was the principal freight locoshed and could play host to a wide range of home based and visiting engines. This is ex-LNWR Webb 5ft 2P 'Watford' 0-6-2T No. 6869. These were introduced in 1898 for local services from Euston and Broad Street until displaced by electrification.

LNWR 'Coal tank' 0-6-2T No. 7765. This was allocated BR No. 58917 but was withdrawn in February 1950 without receiving this.

Another LNWR loco, Webb 18in Goods 0-6-0 No. 8442, later 28442. Allocated BR No. 58379 it was withdrawn in 1949 without receiving this.

Rather more unexpected was this Aspinall 3F 0-6-0 of Lancashire & Yorkshire Rly origin, No 12201. Apparently some of this class were allocated here at the time. This loco was to survive with British Railways as No. 52201 until 1961.

The 2-6-4T design had been introduced to the LMS by Sir Henry Fowler in 1927, and was further developed by Stanier, then Fairburn and eventually Riddles as a BR standard type. Stanier two-cylinder design No. 2539 stands by the coaling tower. These locos would be used on the outer suburban stopping trains to Bletchley, the local service to Watford having been electrified with the third rail system.

Until Stanier's arrival, the standard LMS freight loco was the Fowler 4F 0-6-0, derived from a Midland Railway design. A total of 192 were inherited from the Midland, and a further 580 were built for the LMS from 1924 to 1941. No. 4064 dates from 1925.

Stanier introduced his 'Black Five' 4-6-0 in 1934. The design was continued by British Railways (including a number of variant versions) until a total of 842 were built. They were highly successful engines and lasted until the very end of main line steam. No. 5293 was built in 1936.

Hughes/Fowler 'Crab' 2-6-0 No. 2813 of 1929. Between 1926 and 1932 a total of 245 of these engines was built at Horwich and Crewe works. Designed by George Hughes, formerly of the Lancashire & Yorkshire Railway, but who had been succeeded by Henry Fowler (ex-Midland) by the time construction started. Fowler substituted Midland boiler fittings and a Midland style tender, which was narrower than the cab. The high running board gave these engines an appearance of rugged power.

'Patriot' No. 5509. Unnamed at this time, it later became *The Derbyshire Yeomanry*.

The LNWR 0-8-0 freight engines of class G1 and G2 were considered a successful design, and the G2s outlasted all the other LNWR designs. The G1s went between 1948–52, but some G2s lasted until 1964. This G2, No. 9036, was withdrawn in 1949.

By contrast G2 class No. 9304 was to last until 1959 as BR No. 49304. Ex-LNWR locos never normally carried smokebox number plates under LMS or BR ownership, apparently because the idea came from their arch rivals the Midland Railway.

Great Western

An unidentified Churchward 'Star' class 4-6-0 at Paddington platform 1.

A 'Hall' class, possibly No. 4967 *Shirenewton Hall*. The location is believed to be near Aldermaston.

A 'Castle' class at speed with an express. The location is uncertain but may be Taplow.

48XX No. 4813 stands at Pershore station on a Great Malvern–Honeybourne working. The auto-trailer is one of those converted from one of the original 1903–4 steam railmotors. Seventy-five of these 0-4-2T engines were built between 1932–6 for push-pull working, replacing older locomotives of similar layout.

Reg favoured the cutting just east of Iver station. This was long before the M25 crossed the line here of course! An unidentified 'Hall' class speeds towards London.

Although introduced in 1927, the 'Kings' remained as the principal GWR express motive power until nationalisation. On the same day, this appears to be No. 6016 *King Edward V*.

Although the 'Castle' class predated the 'Kings', they were to outlast the later class with further examples being built by British Railways. This is probably No. 4084 *Aberystwyth Castle* on a down train, in 1938.

'Castle' class No. 4083 *Abbotsbury Castle* on an up train to Paddington in 1938.

Churchward 'Saint' class 4-6-0 No. 2908 *Lady of Quality* on a vans train.

The GWR chose the 2-6-2T for suburban passenger duties. Various sizes were produced with the 61XX being introduced in 1931 by Collett for London suburban duties. No. 6108 is routed over the fast lines in this view.

A Churchward 43XX 2-6-0 either No. 9313 or 9318 works a freight train at Saunderton on the climb through the Chilterns in 1937.

Another 2-6-0, another freight, slogs its way up through the Chilterns.

Churchward introduced the first British 2-8-0 design as far back as 1903 and they continued to be built by his successor Collett. One of the Churchward examples without a side window to the cab, No. 2850 is making steady progress with another long freight in 1938.

The 'Hall' class 4-6-0s were a mixed traffic design, and one is seen here at Saunderton on a stopping passenger turn. This is probably No. 5964 *Wolseley Hall*.

The route up through High Wycombe was the GW & GC Joint, so LNER trains from Marylebone could also be seen here. B17 No. 2867 *Bradford* heads this train on Saunderton bank. The B17s arrived on the GC Section from 1936, and these were paired with a standard LNER 4,200 gallon tender rather than the short GER type. They replaced ex-GCR C4 Atlantics. By summer 1937 all 25 'Footballers' as well as some earlier B17s were all on the GC section. Later on, A3s and V2s replaced them and they were transferred to East Anglia.

The Southern

An LSWR M7 0-4-4T, No. 44, stands at Exeter Central. These engines remained in service on the same branch line duties well into the 1960s.

An SECR Wainwright E class 4-4-0, No. 1587, built in 1907, on a Kent coast train at Hildenborough, between Sevenoaks and Tonbridge in 1937.

One of the smaller railways absorbed into the Southern was the Plymouth, Devonport & South Western Junction Railway. Ex-PD & SWJR 0-6-0T No. 756 *A.S. Harris* became a pilot loco at Nine Elms locoshed where it is seen here. It had been built in 1907 by Hawthorn Leslie and was to survive the Southern Railway, lasting until 1951.

A visit to Stewarts Lane depot produced a variety of loco classes, including this SECR C class 0-6-0, No. 1575.

Also present was H class 0-4-4T No. 1312. A Wainwright design for the SECR, these were introduced in 1904. Sixty-four passed to British Railways.

4-4-0 No. 1078 stands in spotless condition at Stewarts Lane depot. This was one of the F1 class designed by James Stirling in 1886 for the South Eastern Railway and rebuilt by Wainwright for the SECR in 1903. This particular engine was to last until March 1949.

D1 class 4-4-0 No. 1489. The D1s were a Maunsell rebuild of the Wainwright D class of 1901 for the SE&CR.

More modern express power in the form of 'King Arthur' class 4-6-0 No. 771 *Sir Sagramore.* This has an eight-wheeled tender fitted.

Another 'King Arthur', No. 794 *Sir Ector de Maris*, but paired with a six-wheel tender.

The 'Schools' class were built for the Hastings line with its restricted clearances. This is No. 928 *Stowe*, one of three of the class that now survives in preservation.

The N15X 4-6-0s were a rebuild of Billington's Baltic tank engines for the LB&SCR, made redundant after the Brighton line was electrified. This is No. 2330 *Cudworth.*

The most powerful motive power on the Southern at this time were the 'Lord Nelson' 4-6-0s. No 861 *Lord Anson* was on shed on this occasion.

WARTIME GREAT WESTERN IN NORTH WALES

Sapper with a Camera – Recollections of the Second World War

When war was declared in 1939, it looked as if my photographic activities would have to be suspended. Photography began to be discouraged, or in some cases restricted, being viewed with suspicion as possible spying. As the war progressed, leisure travel was to be actively discouraged; the railways being hard-pressed to meet wartime demands. 'Is your journey really necessary?' exhorted a well-known wartime poster.

Being a compositor in the printing trade, I was classified as being in a 'restricted' occupation at first and so not conscripted; but the rules were changed and I received my call-up papers at the age of 27 in March 1941. Although I am an East Londoner my military career started in Wales for I was first drafted to the Royal Army Ordnance Corps at Pembroke Dock. This involved a journey I can remember nothing about except that it seemed to take forever! Perhaps the 'Great' in 'Great Western' referred to the distances it covered!

After military training I was then sent to Croydon as a draughtsman. This was ironic, as I had earlier applied for a post as draughtsman with the LNER at Stratford Works, only to be turned down on medical grounds after a trial period. When I arrived back at Paddington, it was to be told that the dining room at the Mitcham Road barracks had been set on fire by incendiary bombs during the night. So the authorities decided that we should go to the Great Central Hotel at Marylebone. Here we would spend the night sleeping on the floor, then have breakfast and proceed to Croydon in the morning.

My first two years of service saw my transfer to the Royal Engineers, with a posting at Ashford amongst other places. I was involved in producing drawings for the 25-pounder gun, which was introduced in 1943, and mobile expanding workshops for General Montgomery's desert campaign.

Later, I was moved on again. Now I was to be posted to 250 Field Company in Norfolk, where our unit was located alongside the LNER Norwich–Yarmouth line at Brundall Gardens near Norwich. We were told we were to undergo intensive battlefield training prior to being posted overseas.

One day we were being given a demonstration of setting explosives with gun cotton primers and a ring main circuit. You took a long length of flex and set the gun cotton primers at regular intervals. The ring main was packed with mud so as not to lose velocity. The officer in charge picked on me, stating that I had not been paying attention to what he had been explaining (well I had had one eye on the railway!) "Batten, you're not paying attention. Now get out here and demonstrate to the platoon what I've been talking about." So I did exactly that, and stated that having placed and connected the primers in contact with the exploders you gently pressed the exploder lever down, and finally gave it a jerk, accompanying my words with the appropriate actions.

The explosive charge detonated with an almighty bang, doing extensive damage to the adjacent level crossing! There were pieces of wood flying everywhere. The officer was furious. He hadn't intended for the explosives to be set off for real but was too late to stop me. Of course he judged me responsible. "I'm putting you on a charge!" he shouted. "It's not my fault," I retorted, "I did what you ordered, you should have made sure the exploder was disconnected."

Well, I was put on a charge, and had to attend a court martial at Britannia Barracks. Naturally I was pretty apprehensive, and my colleagues weren't exactly comforting. "They could shoot you for this!" somebody told me. But I was determined to make my case that it was not my fault. I told them that I had demonstrated the procedure exactly as the officer has described it. It was the officer's responsibility to make sure that the exploder was disconnected. Luckily my plea was accepted, and

I was told to my relief that I was admonished. Instead the officer was charged with failing to ensure the safety of the men under his command.*

I had now been rated 'Category B3', which meant I did not see service abroad but had various postings and locations scattered throughout the United Kingdom.

A later posting was to Ripon, Yorkshire. When I arrived there, I was told that I was being sent on a course as a military photographer, which I passed satisfactorily. I was placed on headquarters staff, in the survey department, with six others. Here I used a Leica III series and a half plate field camera. Part of my work involved processing aerial reconnaissance photographs for the RAF. Some of these films were several feet long, and were developed by a see-saw method, dipping in and out of large dishes on the floor.

About once every six weeks you were granted a weekend 48-hour pass, which allowed me to get home to see my parents. On one occasion when I had such a pass, I decided to travel from Thirsk, on the East Coast Main Line where I could catch a train to King's Cross which was due to arrive around 6am, thus enjoying a longer weekend at home. When the train arrived at Thirsk it was already packed to capacity. There were troops and civilians alike standing in the corridors and even some sleeping in the luggage racks. I got in with all my gear – pack, gas mask, rifle etc. and a seated man in 'civvies' saw me struggling to get in and said: "You look tired friend, with all that equipment. Have you come far?"

"Ripon," I replied.

"Going far?"

"East London," I said, "to see my parents."

"That's a fair way," he said, "Tell you what, you share this seat with me in turns and that will be easier for both of us." I thanked him for his generosity and this we then did. On arrival at King's Cross, some hours later, we bade our farewells and parted.

When I reached the barrier and the ticket collector asked to see my pass, I reached inside the pocket of my greatcoat for my wallet. It was gone! Pass, money, ration card for the weekend, the lot – pickpocketed, stolen.

I had some loose change to allow me to get home and the military police helped me with a temporary pass so as to avoid further trouble. They also told me to give a statement to the police. This I did but they were rather dismissive. I was informed that what I had had the misfortune to suffer was rife and going on all the time. They said as they had a bullion train coming in they were not interested in trifles like mine!

So I had been conned and robbed, and it made for a miserable 48-hour break. It disgusted me that people could take advantage of wartime conditions to rob the very people who were supposed to be fighting to keep them in a free country. Still at least if I got through the war losing nothing more than my money, I could count myself lucky compared to many poor buggers.

In 1943 after undergoing a course as an armourer, I was assigned to Ruabon in North Wales as unit armourer. We were quartered at Wynnstay Hall, the estate of Sir William Watkins Wynn. Although I did not know so then, I was to serve the rest of my war years here until we were eventually demobbed in 1946.

Before the war I had been a keen photographer of railways (though mainly of my native LNER), and the countryside. Now that I was being posted to all these new and interesting places, many of which I would not have otherwise had the opportunity or money to visit, I was determined to continue the practice, if possible! I soon found a suitable solution. Being unit armourer meant that I had a comprehensive set of tools. I took full advantage of this and kept my camera at the bottom of the green-baize lined toolbox. The key to this was kept in the guardroom, and except for the RSM, I had sole access. When off duty I could collect my camera and carry it in a pocket of my battledress intended for a field dressing. Army life wasn't all work. I had considerable free time in which to pursue my two loves of railways and the countryside. During that time, I spent many happy hours by the lineside.

A suitably remote and photogenic location I made use of various occasions was Cefn Mawr, near Ruabon. I saw various standard GWR types here such as 'Granges' and 53XX 2-6-0s. Heavy freight trains were

---

* It was only many years after this article was published that Reg revealed the true nature of this story. The officer in charge had expressed a dislike of Londoners, and as the only cockney in the unit, Reg had borne the full brunt of his disapproval and bullying. Reg had seen the officer disconnect the exploder. When his back was turned, he seized the opportunity and quickly reconnected it, anticipating the subsequent consequences!

commonplace. There were also local stopping trains, provided mainly for the miners at the then thriving collieries around Wrexham. These tended to be 48XX 0-4-2Ts with autotrailers.

I also travelled all over the local area, sometimes by train or bus to Llangollen, but mainly on foot. I walked for miles along roads and over the hills. Army life kept you fit! My boots always seemed to get worn out before anyone else's!

On other occasions I travelled further afield by train to Gobowen, Oswestry etc. I also managed journeys to Barmouth (officially out of bounds to us troops) and to Bala, along the now-closed continuation of the Llangollen Railway. Many towns, including Wrexham and Oswestry, had branches of the WVS where I could get a refreshing meal.

About once every six weeks, we had a 48-hour pass weekend leave. I did not consider it practical to try heading all the way home to the East End of London. For one thing, with all the bombing that London was getting, I could not guarantee that I would be able to get back in time. Instead I would travel to Chester or Shrewsbury and stay there overnight. Troops could get a B&B for around one shilling. At Chester you could get a slap-up meal. No bombs ever fell on Chester, and at times there you would hardly know that there was a war on.

However, sometimes things took a more serious turn, and not necessarily as a consequence of Hitler's activities. On the evening of 6 September 1945, following an extensive period of heavy rain, the Shropshire Union Canal burst its banks between Llangollen and Ruabon, washing away the earthworks of the adjacent railway, and leaving the track suspended in mid-air. Unfortunately, a mail and goods train, hauled by 2-6-0 No. 6315, arrived on the scene before the damage was noted and was derailed, plunging down the bank. Our unit was called out to help make good the damage, but neither we nor the GWR could do anything to lift the loco and it was eventually cut up on site.

Wartime photography was not just a matter of smuggling a camera into army camp. Although private photography was not actually forbidden, the taking of pictures showing war-related activities was prohibited. The railways were playing a crucial role moving troops and munitions, so were regarded as of strategic importance. Therefore the production of a camera was likely to be challenged by the authorities.

Although I was in military uniform, this did not entitle me to be on the line or exempt me from any restrictions on photography. In practice, I never had any problems from either loco crews or track and signalling staff – they probably thought I was there to guard the railway installations! Places like Cefn Mawr near Ruabon were sufficiently remote from the authorities, as were some of my favourite locations when on home leave, such as Potters Bar and Saunderton near High Wycombe. But I did not try to use my camera in London or any other cities.

Taking photographs of buildings could also cause problems. Seemingly innocuous manor houses might have been requisitioned for military purposes. On one occasion, when on leave and in 'civvies', I was arrested near Cheshunt, Herts while taking pictures. Not satisfied with my explanations, the police took me before the local army commandant. When ordered to show my identity papers, I produced my identity AB64 army documents and claimed I was on intelligence business, whereupon I was released and invited to take a meal in the camp canteen!

Furthermore, I made no attempt to keep written records of locos seen or photos taken. Any such notebook, if found by the civil or military police, might well be construed as spying, and protestations of innocence not believed. Better safe than sorry!

Photographic trips were not always successful. One particular foray I recall was a disaster from start to finish for a number of bizarre reasons. Whilst stationed at Ripon I decided one free Saturday to visit the town of Knaresborough. There is a charming view of the town with the railway bridge over the River Nidd in the foreground and the church in the background – a view I had sometimes seen in the *Railway Magazine* and wished to try for myself. As a lifelong Gresley fan I also wished to take the D49 'Hunts' and 'Shires' that operated in this area. I boarded the bus at Ripon, and all seemed well until the bus suddenly lurched to one side, skirted a ditch, and ended up in a field. There were no injuries but we were kept waiting till a relief bus arrived to take us onwards.

I had started walking over the fields towards the river and railway bridge when I was apprehended by several soldiers of another corps, Royal Signals, and taken under escort before their commanding officer. They were engaged on an exercise, and as a member of a different unit (RE) and out of bounds in their area,

I was an 'enemy'. I was taken 'prisoner' and although well fed, was held until 4.00pm. By then the light was unsuitable for photography, so I went to the cinema before returning to Ripon for lights out.

For the would-be wartime photographer, legal restrictions were not the only limiting factor. There was the problem of obtaining the necessary film and other equipment. Film could not be bought openly. I could only obtain 120 size film on home leave from my friends at Kodak, in Kingsway, who kept some 'under the counter', or at other shops where I was known. Chemicals and paper were also in short supply, although boxes of American-made 5 x 5in paper were sold on the black market.

VE Day came while I was still based at Ruabon. This was to be a day for relaxing and celebrating. Correctly surmising that restrictions would not be enforced on this, of all days, I decided to 'bunk' the GWR locoshed at Oswestry. As well as the standard fare of GWR locomotives, Oswestry was home to some unusual ex-Cambrian Railway veteran 2-4-0Ts. These were required to work the Tanat Valley Light Railway, which ran to Llangynog and was subject to a weight restriction. Fortunately for me, three of these interesting engines were to be found lined up, and clear of obstructing locomotives – just waiting to be photographed! Later in the

day, we were entertained by the WVS, and all food and drink was supplied free to the troops.

With the end of hostilities, it became possible once more to take photographs openly. But of course I was still in service so my travelling opportunities afield were restricted to weekend passes. Supplies of photographic equipment did not get back to normal for some time either.

When demobilisation came, it was to take place at Taunton. In preparation for this our unit moved to Longleat House near Warminster. When the long-awaited day finally came, we were taken by lorry to Warminster station to catch the train to Taunton. When this came, to my surprise it was formed by one of the GWR diesel railcars – a new experience for me. This stopped at all stations to Taunton, an interesting if somewhat tedious journey. After I had been fitted out with 'civvies' and had a meal, I came back behind No. 5013 *Abergavenny Castle*, first stop Westbury – which was more like it!

I handed in my army gear and left for home and 'civvy street' back to London (and LNER territory!) behind another 'Castle', fast to Paddington, with only a stop at Reading. My five and a half years of National Service were over, and I was many rolls of film the richer for it. My only regret was that I didn't keep any records of the dates on which I took the photographs.

GWR 'Saint' class 4-6-0 No. 2930 *Saint Vincent* on a Chester–Shrewsbury express at Cefn Mawr, a few miles south of Ruabon. Unusually for 1945, this was in clean condition at the time.

'Grange' class No. 6868 *Penrhos Grange* on a long mixed freight.

Another 'Grange', too dirty to be identified.

'Hall' class
No. 5966 *Ashford Hall*
with a fitted freight.

'Hall' No. 6950
Kingsthorpe Hall hurries
a passenger train.

An up passenger train, worked by an unidentifiable 'Hall' class 4-6-0. Wartime conditions left many locomotives too grimy for the numbers to be visible.

48XX 0-4-2T No. 4801 with an autotrain. These trains were used by the miners travelling to work at the local collieries at Gresford etc.

48XX No. 4811 with another autotrain.

A passenger train crosses the viaduct near Chirk. The canal aqueduct is visible behind the viaduct.

A view of the Chirk railway viaduct, taken from the top of the parallel canal aqueduct. What is probably a 'Castle' class 4-6-0 is passing over on a passenger train. The viaduct carries the Great Western Railway main line from Shrewsbury to Chester. This view has not changed over the intervening years, although the trains will be different of course!

GWR No. 819, formerly named *Eadweade*. No. 819 was a Hunslet 0-6-0T originally built for the Lambourn Valley Railway in 1903. It was sold to the Cambrian Railway in 1904, becoming No. 24, and passed in turn to the GWR. Seen at Oswestry shed in 1945, it was used on the 15-mile long Tanat Valley line that ran from Llynclys Junction near Oswestry to Llangynog and which was of single track construction laid with lightweight flat-bottom rails. The line was severely restricted to a 12ton 10cwt limit. This precluded such types as the 48XX (later 14XX) 0-4-2T and necessitated the continued use of 2-4-0T types and this light 0-6-0T. The track was eventually relaid in 1946, after which the restrictions were relaxed and the veterans were withdrawn.

GWR No. 1196 was one of a pair of 2-4-0T built for the Cambrian Railway by Sharp Stewart, Manchester in 1866 and rebuilt in 1894. The Cambrian Railway gave them the numbers 58–59, becoming 1196–97 under the GWR. No. 1196 was transferred to Exeter in 1927, and here it worked on the Culm Valley branch. However, it was returned to Oswestry at the end of 1928. Withdrawal came in April 1948, with scrapping the following month.

Great Western Railway 2-4-0T No. 1308 *Lady Margaret* taken on shed at Oswestry on VE Day 1945. This was built by Andrew Barclay in 1907 for the Liskeard & Looe Rly. After acquisition by the GWR it went to Swindon where it received a Dean type boiler and other Great Western fittings. It ran for a few more years on the Looe branch before being transferred north to Oswestry. Here it worked on the Tanat Valley Light Railway along with the two older ex-Cambrian Rly Sharp Stewart 2-4-0Ts. It was cut up in 1948.

POST-WAR DAYS

LNER – The Run-Down Years around Potters Bar 1946–7

During the war the railways had taken a real battering and the tracks were in no fit state for high-speed running for some time to come. There were no streamliners or non-stop trains at first, and journey times were longer than pre-war. It was not until the autumn of 1949, when the 'North Briton' was booked for the 44.1 miles from Darlington to York in 44 minutes, that any BR train was scheduled for mile-a-minute running. It was to be 1951 before any part of the ECML, that pre-war racing track, was passed for 90mph running.

Typifying the condition of many locomotives after the war, an A3, too grimy to be identified, heads an express passenger train near Potters Bar, probably in 1947.

Even the A4s, the pride of the LNER, were not exempted. This is No. 29 *Woodcock* at the same location. The valances over the wheels were removed during the war for ease of maintenance and were not reinstated. Under the renumbering of LNER locos in 1943, the A4s took numbers 1–34. There had been one other member of the class but No. 4469 *Sir Ralph Wedgwood* (originally *Gadwall*) was the unfortunate victim destroyed in an air raid at York station in April 1942, along with B16 No. 925.

Edward Thompson controversially rebuilt the prototype Gresley Pacific No. 4470 *Great Northern* (then still an A1) in 1945. Now classified as class A1/1, the locomotive is seen in its later rebuilt form with smoke deflectors and standard cab sides in 1946. At this stage it retains its original number but would become No. 113 in October that year. Under British Railways it would become No. 60113. It was withdrawn at the end of 1962. Note the electric lights fitted, rather than the customary oil lamps. This photograph made the front cover of the May/June 1948 *Railway Magazine*.

The V2s were sometimes called 'the engines that won the war'. Equally at home with passenger or fast freight work they performed admirably, with loads far in excess of what they had been intended to tackle. Here one passes the drain at Potters Bar on a passenger turn.

Another unidentifiable V2 – another passenger working. An everyday scene in the early post-war years.

The winter of 1946 was particularly severe. V2 No. 850 heads the 3.40pm 'Scotch Goods' through a snowbound Potters Bar cutting.

New on the scene were the Thompson B1 4-6-0s, introduced in 1942 and still being constructed at this time. They were very much the LNER equivalent of Stanier's 'Black Five' on the rival LMS. They could be found on passenger and freight turns, including suburban trains that did not proceed via the 'Widened Lines' to Moorgate. No. 1089, new in 1946, is on such a train on the same day.

The N2s remained the mainstay of suburban workings. No. 9529 heads a customary pair of 'quad-arts'. No question of suspending services due to snowy conditions in those days!

The B17 4-6-0s could be found on Cambridge line trains, from which they had displaced Atlantics since 1932. This is No. 1624 *Lumley Castle* in 1947. Note the clerestory roof carriage at the front of the train.

Still carrying its old number is K3 2-6-0 No. 2761 on a passenger working.

The Ivatt Atlantics were still around but would not last much longer. Withdrawals had started in 1943. Seventeen of the class passed to British Railways in 1948 but all would be withdrawn by the end of 1950. No. 2879 is on a stopping service for Hitchin or Cambridge – a role from which they would be displaced by the new B1s.

Freight traffic remained the lifeblood of the railways, and here a Robinson O4 2-8-0 heads a lengthy mixed freight train. These locos were chosen as a wartime standard during the First World War.

An unusual sight in the London area was this Raven NER B16/1 4-6-0 No. 1459 on a long train of fitted vans, probably the 'Scotch Goods'. It was possibly substituting for a failed V2.

The Riddles 'Austerity' 2-8-0 was designed for the Ministry of Supply in 1943 for the Railway Operating Division of the War Department. Two hundred were acquired by the LNER in 1946 as class O7, and allocated numbers 3000–3199. Still carrying its ROD number 78642, this was allocated LNER No. 3135. Here it heads a train of coal wagons in 1947.

Another WD 2-8-0, too grimy to be identified, with another rake of coal wagons.

Another WD 2-8-0, this time with a train of bogie bolster wagons, perhaps carrying rails. This also displays a painted ROD number on the smokebox which appears to be 78886.

Representing an earlier design of heavy freight loco, K3 2-6-0 No. 1885 bursts from Potters Bar tunnel with a covered vans train.

A Gresley K2 2-6-0, filthy and with a missing cylinder cover, but otherwise apparently steaming well, heads another train of covered vans.

LNER at Shenfield 1945–6

N7 0-6-2T No. 2618 leaves Shenfield on an up train to Liverpool Street composed of a Gresley 'quint-art' plus four other coaches. The locomotive is leaking badly and making hard work of its train.

A grimy J39 0-6-0 heads a train near Shenfield on the Great Eastern Line from London Liverpool Street.

D16/3 4-4-0 No. 8821 is seen with a rather mixed rake of carriages.

A wartime view of LNER rebuilt D16/3 No. 8899 on a Southend to Liverpool Street service leaving Shenfield. The loco is dirty, leaking and making hard work of it.

Post-war Southern Railway

A grubby, unidentified 'Lord Nelson' passes Wimbledon with a down express for Southampton.

Bulleid's 'Merchant Navy' Pacifics were introduced during the war years. Again at Wimbledon, 21C15 *Rotterdam Lloyd* heads an up express for London Waterloo.

To justify their construction during wartime, Bulleid's Pacifics were described as being mixed traffic locomotives. Here 'Battle of Britain' light Pacific 21C152 *Lord Dowding* heads a milk train of empties away from London.

The former London & South Western Railway had introduced third rail electrification to some of their suburban lines, while the London, Brighton & South Coast had opted for overhead wires. The Southern chose the LSWR system and extended this to much of their suburban network and some of the main lines to the south coast during the 1920s and 1930s, replacing the overhead network. Electric Multiple Unit No. 1430 is typical of the stock used on the local services.

Another train, headed by four-car unit 4490, heads south at Wimbledon. Note the second coach is of a more modern all steel construction.

'Lord Nelson', No. 864 *Sir Martin Frobisher* at speed with a boat train on the LSWR main line from Waterloo. The location is believed to be either Byfleet or West Byfleet in 1947.

At the same location is 'King Arthur' No. 766 *Sir Geraint* with a train bound for Bournemouth West, according to the head-code discs.

N15X 4-6-0 No. 2329 *Stephenson* heads a train with some rather ancient looking coaches – probably a relief train. The Southern used a series of headcode discs to indicate the route taken, rather than the usual lamp codes. The single disc here indicates a train from Waterloo to Southampton Terminus but not a boat train.

H15 class 4-6-0 No. 484. The headcode discs suggest this is another train for Bournemouth. This was a Urie design for the LSWR, dating from 1914.

An elderly ex-LSWR Drummond T14 'Paddlebox' 4-6-0 No. 461 has charge of a milk train, probably the same service as seen before, with *Lord Dowding* working it on that occasion. This was the last member of the class to be withdrawn, in June 1951.

Belgian Holiday

At some stage during the late 1940s Reg went on holiday to Belgium, visiting Ostend, Bruges and Ghent. Although he was principally photographing buildings, he did take some pictures of trains at the stations, mainly in Ghent.

American built 2-8-0 No. 29227 at Gent (Ghent). Three hundred of these were supplied in 1945–6 under the Marshall plan to revive the Belgian railway network. One example, 29013, has been preserved.

4-6-0 No. 62012 arrives at Ghent.

4-6-0 No. 62012 at
the terminus beside
2-8-0 No. 29227.

4-6-0 No. 62012 at Gent St Pieters.

An elderly 0-6-0 heads some equally ancient looking coaches.

Semi-streamlined Pacific No. 1020, possibly at Ostend.

INTO NATIONALISATION

LNER/BR around Potters Bar 1947–9

Gradually things began to improve, as track, locomotive and rolling stock repairs were undertaken. Cleanliness returned so that once again engines were identifiable! A3 Pacific No. 48 *Doncaster* is looking quite presentable on this occasion. No lining is evident, so this is maybe painted in wartime black. It would be repainted from black to green in June 1947.

Next numerically is No. 49 *Galtee More*. Not so clean, but at least identifiable. This had regained green livery in December 1946.

Nationalisation in 1948 saw LNER engines having the number 60,000 added to their existing numbers. Now as 60054, *Prince of Wales* has British Railways spelled out on the tender side. This had been built as an A1 class in 1924, as No. 2553 *Manna*. It was renamed in 1926, the original name later carried by another engine which became BR No. 60085. It was rebuilt as an A3 in 1943.

British Railways tried various liveries before standardising on lined Brunswick green for passenger engines. For a while class 7 and 8 engines were painted in blue and it looks as if A3 No. 60096 *Papyrus* is so painted in this view of it working the Yorkshire Pullman. It carried BR blue livery from August 1949 until April 1952. Note also the original version of the lion and wheel emblem. The train had been withdrawn during the war but was reinstated in November 1946.

A4 Pacific No. 28 *Walter K. Whigham* passes under the drain.

The A4s were not numbered in age order. One of the original 1935 batch, No. 15 *Quicksilver*, emerges from Potters Bar tunnel. We saw this before in pre-war days as No. 2510.

British Railways A4 No. 60034 *Lord Farringdon*. Until February 1948 this had been named *Peregrine*, but it was renamed when the ex-GCR B7 which previously bore the name was withdrawn (see photo page 23).

Thompson introduced his A2/3 Pacifics in 1946 following his rebuilding of Gresley's P2 2-8-2s to 4-6-2 Pacifics. Numerically the first and running as BR No. E500 is *Edward Thompson*. Note the double chimney.

Class A2/3 No. 60513 *Dante,* one of the production batch built in 1946.

LNER A2/3 No. 523 *Sun Castle* has charge of the 'Yorkshire Pullman'. From 1949 this was an eleven-coach train, with sections from Harrogate, Hull, Leeds and Bradford.

This is one of the 'Peppercorn' 1947 development of the A2 class, with a shorter wheelbase. The number is partly obscured but the loco may be 60533 *Happy Knight*, built in 1948.

A.H. Peppercorn introduced his own A1 Pacifics but none of these were delivered until after nationalisation. They shared the 6ft 8in driving wheels and three-cylinder layout of the classic Gresley Pacifics. The cylinders at 19in x 26in were of similar dimensions to those of the A3s. However, the boiler pressure was increased from 220psi on the A3s to 250psi on the A1s, i.e. similar to that of the A4s. BR No. 60128, built in 1949 and still unnamed at this stage, is working the 'West Riding'. It is painted in BR blue but seems to have a coat of grime – not ideal for a named train! It would be named *Bongrace* in November 1950. The post-war 'West Riding' introduced in 1949 ran between Leeds/Bradford and London, non-stop from Wakefield to King's Cross.

The first of the A1 class No. 60114 *W.P. Allen* is in the lined blue livery in which many of the class were delivered new.

An A1 or A2 Pacific crosses the Digswell viaduct at Welwyn.

B1 4-6-0 No. 1107 on a stopping train in 1947.

B1 4-6-0 No. 1136 on fitted freight passing under the drain.

With all the new
A1 Pacifics and B1
4-6-0s about, the
B17 4-6-0s were
redeployed to
humbler duties.
No. 61633 *Kimbolton
Castle* is on suburban
stock of 'quad-art'
articulated coaches.

Doyen of the V2s,
No. 800 *Green Arrow*
also finds itself on an
outer suburban stop-
ping service.

This V2 is just about identifiable as No. 60862 from its front number plate. Of interest is that this train has the former 'Silver Jubilee' triplet dining coaches in its formation – just visible beyond the drain.

The condensing N2 0-6-2Ts remained the mainstay of suburban workings from Moorgate. BR No. 69587 works a train to Hatfield.

BR No. 69493 drifts along with a local train for Welwyn Garden City.

LNER No. 9537 bursts out of Potters Bar tunnel on another local train for Welwyn Garden City.

'Cherry Blossom' and his Beloved N2

When I was demobbed from the Royal Engineers in March 1946, I lost little time in resuming my photographic activities, particularly on the East Coast main line around my favourite location of Potters Bar.

It was during this period that I made the acquaintance of driver John Hutchins of King's Cross shed. A ruddy-faced man with a jovial and kindly attitude, his pride and joy was his regular engine, class N2/4 0-6-2T No. 9571, with left-hand drive. He used to keep this locomotive in pristine condition, so much so that he could often be found at the shed on his rest days, cleaning and polishing the cab fittings and controls to his personal satisfaction! Hence his nickname 'Cherry Blossom', after his complexion and the popular boot polish of that name (although I don't know if he actually applied that to the N2!).

He frequently worked on the Hertford North trains, and during this period he befriended a young boy who was about ten years old and who used to help out with odd jobs at Cuffley & Goffs Oak station. Driver Hutchins honoured him with at least three footplate rides on the Hertford line.

Some years later I met this lad (whose name I have now forgotten) and he told me how, on one of these footplate trips, Driver Hutchins did not have his usual 9571 but instead had a right-hand drive N2/2 in its place. He decided to see if it was as good as his regular mount. He departed Hertford at what seemed like full regulator and full cut-off, and halfway up the bank to Bayford, the fireman (again, I believe, not his regular one) turned to the lad puffing and panting, his face streaming with perspiration, and said "What is he trying to do, kill me?" My friend said how he wished that he had been older and had had a stopwatch at the time, as the timings might have been really something to savour. I guess Driver Hutchins decided the N2/2 was OK, although he probably told the other drivers that it wouldn't steam for toffee and was not a patch on his beloved 9571!

There used to be a bit of a wager amongst some drivers as to whether anyone could run through Ponsbourne tunnel, between Cuffley and Bayford, which is 1 mile 924 yards long, in one minute. I don't know if it was ever achieved, but I sometimes wonder if 'Cherry Blossom' ever managed it – if he didn't it was probably not for the lack of trying.

Unfortunately Driver Hutchins died shortly afterwards, as result of a sudden heart attack, like Sir Nigel Gresley a few years earlier.

A J39 0-6-0, No. 64729, at the head of a mixed freight.

The 200 WD 2-8-0s of LNER class O7 did not all take up their intended BR numbers of 63000–63199, as they were instead numbered 90000–90100 and 90422–90520. A further 533 locos were acquired by British Railways from the War Department. This unidentified example is on the typical unfitted coal train that these locos were most associated with throughout their lifetime. Note that the Westinghouse brake pump has been removed.

LNER/BR in East Anglia

Chasing Steam in East Anglia

Like most working-class people at the time, before and after the war I could not afford a car. However, my brother and I were the proud owners of a racing tandem. We would use this to take holiday or weekend breaks, covering hundreds of miles in the process. Sometimes we would head up from our home in London to Norwich (via Cambridge or Ipswich) where we would stay overnight.

Our objective was visiting and photographing the Broads, and the picturesque villages and churches of the surrounding area; but any local railway interest was not to be ignored! Many towns and villages were served by branch lines, now but a memory, so there was a good chance of meeting up with a line. A 'pulled-off' signal visible from a bridge, or a closed set of level crossing gates merited investigation. The resulting train would very likely be hauled by a venerable ex-GER loco, often one of the ubiquitous J15 0-6-0s.

Sometimes, however, the railway photographs were the consequence of unforeseen circumstances, as in the following incident. On one excursion to the Ipswich area in July 1947 we set out to photograph the church at Great Blakenham, Suffolk. Walking round the churchyard I decided the best vantage point for my picture would be from standing on top of a dung heap! But as I took my photo I felt a sharp pain in my right leg and realised that I had been stung. We were both wearing shorts on this hot day. As we headed back to the village my leg grew painful and inflamed, and a swelling appeared about the size of a small egg. Seeing a barber's shop I thought I might be able to get an antiseptic salve.

I limped in and asked the barber if he could 'put me out of my misery'. A customer was being lathered and shaved with a cut-throat razor. Waving his razor at me the barber replied with a grin, "I'm sure we can oblige."

"No, not that, I've been stung," I said.

"Where did that happen then?"

"I was in the churchyard photographing the church."

"Serves you right for desecrating God's acre. Let's have a look at it." Anyway, he supplied a soothing balm and suggested I take it easy for a while till the swelling went down.

I asked him if there were any other old buildings worth photographing in the area and he mentioned a watermill at nearby Baylham which was approached by a bridge spanning the main line from Ipswich to Norwich. However, when we got to the field where the mill was sited there was a sign saying 'Beware of the bull!' and said bull was very visibly present. So I decided to leave the mill and go back to the bridge, climb over, and indulge in a spot of railway photography, at the same time resting my leg, which had begun to get painful again.

We were not to be disappointed, for first to appear was B1 4-6-0 No. 1271, nearly new and resplendent in apple-green livery on a Norwich–London express. Next came E4 2-4-0 No. 2796 on a local train with a very mixed rake of coaches, followed by a J17 0-6-0 on freight. A later express for London was in the hands of the normal motive power at the time, a B17 4-6-0, No. 1668 *Bradford City*.

We headed back to Ipswich, well satisfied with the day's photographs despite the initial setbacks. The location was subsequently revisited, a year or two later, by which time the LNER had become British Railways. After all, I still had a watermill to be photographed!

B17 No. 1629 *Naworth Castle* is departing from Norwich in September 1946.

In LNER apple green, B1 No. 1271 was built in 1947 and would have been almost new when photographed at Baylham Mill that year.

By contrast BR No. 61098 from March locoshed is in BR lined black livery when seen on a repeat visit a year later.

An ex-GER J20 0-6-0, No. 64679, works a local passenger with some antiquated stock.

An ex-GER J17 0-6-0, No. 65534, on a mixed freight train.

A real vintage train! The GER E4 2-4-0 class was destined to be the last of this wheel arrangement with British Railways. Eighteen of the class passed to BR and No. 2796 here lasted until 1957. The last one, BR No. 62785, went in 1959 and was preserved as part of the National Collection.

D16/3 4-4-0 No. 2529 carries British Railways' lettering on its tender but has yet to receive its BR number 62529 or a smokebox number plate.

J20 class 0-6-0 No. 64679 returns on another local passenger train.

Again near Baylham Mill is B17 No. 1668 *Bradford City* on a London-bound express in July 1947.

At the same location and we see B1 No. 1271 again.

Another B1 and this time it is No. 1047.

Still going strong is 'Claud Hamilton' D16/3 No. 62568 believed to be near Tivetshall Junction. The last of the class was No. 62613, withdrawn in October 1960. None were preserved.

'Maids of all work' – a J15 drifts through the Suffolk countryside on a typical local train.

B1 4-6-0 No. 1051 at Keswick crossing, near Cringleford, Norfolk.

The 'Britannia' Pacifics were first allocated to the Liverpool Street–Norwich service in 1951. No. 70012 *John of Gaunt* departs from Witham with a train for Liverpool Street during June 1958.

Another 'Britannia', No. 70037 *Hereward the Wake,* at speed near Hatfield Peveril.

The 'Britannias' replaced the B17s on the principal trains. This is No. 61612 *Houghton Hall* at the same location.

The first English Electric Type 4 diesels (later class 40) were allocated to Stratford in 1958 to replace the 'Britannias' on the Norwich trains. One of these passes through Romford *en route* to Liverpool Street, c. 1959. Front yellow warning panels would not be applied until the 1960s.

A notable feature at Hailsworth station, on the line from Ipswich to Lowestoft, was the section of platform included as part of the level crossing gates. Here the gates are being closed for the arrival of a train. These still remain *in situ* as part of the platform but are no longer opened as a level crossing.

The double-track swing bridge at Oulton Broad South on the East Suffolk line allows marine access. The bridge dates from 1907 when it replaced an earlier single-track structure.

LMS/BR Main Lines from London 1947–9

The doyen of the 'Royal Scots', now BR No. 46100. The nameplate on the smokebox door and the bell presented when the locomotive visited the USA in 1933 are readily visible, here at Bourne End.

Many of the class had been rebuilt with taper boilers from 1943 onwards, and all would be so treated by 1955. Already converted was No. 6147 *The Northamptonshire Regiment*. Smoke deflectors would be added later.

BR No. 46144 *Honourable Artillery Company*.

'Patriot' No. 5544 at Bourne End was one of the few that never carried a name.

Like the 'Royal Scots', some of the 'Patriots' (but not all) were rebuilt with taper boilers, double chimney and new cylinders. No. 45530 *Sir Frank Ree* was one so treated. Here it is paired with a Stanier tender, still lettered 'LMS'.

By contrast, this is 'Jubilee' No. 45673 *Keppel*. There is a strong family resemblance at this time between the 'Jubilees', and the rebuilt 'Royal Scots' and 'Patriots'. This would be lessened when the latter two classes later received smoke deflectors.

Stanier 'Jubilee' No. 5619 *Nigeria* at Elstree on the Midland main line.

Another of the class, No. 5636 *Uganda*. The lighting for photography at Elstree was best on up trains in the morning and down trains in the after-noon, as indeed was also the case at Bourne End.

Stanier's 'Black Five' 4-6-0s could be found throughout the length and breadth of the LMS network. No. 4853 is at Elstree. A horse box is at the front of the train.

The class was equally at home on freight and passenger work and would survive to the very end of British Railways main line steam operations in 1968. No. 4984 is again seen at Elstree.

The Midland Compounds were still in everyday use on the Midland main line, albeit on lighter duties. LMS-built No. 1050 at Elstree is probably on a Bedford semi-fast as it was allocated to Bedford shed into the early 1950s.

Another Compound, believed to be No. 1029, overtakes Fowler 2-6-4T No. 2326 on a local train. No. 1029 was one of the original Midland engines, built in 1906, and was withdrawn in June 1948.

Fowler 2-6-4T No. 2325 with another suburban train.

LMS Stanier 2-6-2T No. 99 seen piloting Fowler equivalent No. 39 working a heavy outer suburban train heading northwards near Elstree, Herts, in June 1946. No. 39 is one of a number that were fitted with condensing apparatus for working through the Metropolitan 'Widened Lines' to Moorgate.

Hughes/Fowler 'Crab' 2-6-0 No. 2816 with a lengthy mixed freight at Elstree. The headlamp code is for an express freight, livestock perishable or ballast train not fitted with continuous brake.

Stanier 8F 2-8-0 No. 8544 heads one of the many coal trains that traversed the Midland main line bringing the black stuff from the Derbyshire and Nottinghamshire coalfields to the capital.

Milk was another important freight traffic, brought up to Cricklewood. 'Patriot' No. 5535 *Sir Herbert Walker KCB* returns the empties. Glass-lined milk tank wagons were first introduced in 1927. These, along with road tankers, replaced the churns as the chief means of distribution. They would either be attached to passenger trains or run as dedicated milk trains. They were six-wheeled in order to provide a smoother ride.

On another day,
the milk empties
are hauled by Class
5 No. 4856.

British Railways 'Crab'
M2767 works tender
first with an engineer-
ing works train. The
'M' prefix to the num-
ber was a temporary
arrangement before
BR numbers were
finalised. The disparity
between the width of
the cab and tender is
evident in this view.

LMS-built Midland Compound No. 1152 on a parcels train.

A vision of the future! The LMS ordered two main line locomotives in 1946 for comparison with steam propulsion and there was considerable pressure to have at least one in service before nationalisation took place. The mechanical parts were constructed at Derby, with the engine, traction motors and other electrical equipment supplied by English Electric. No. 10000 was completed in December 1947, with its sister, No. 10001 appearing in July 1948. They were painted in black with silver band and bogies, but only 10000 carried the LMS initials (in cast aluminium letters). No. 10000 was seen here at Elstree in 1948. From April 6 it was working two round trips daily from London to Derby, making a total of 3,084 miles scheduled over a six-day week. Performance was considered satisfactory, with the locomotive having power and time in hand on the 'Jubilee' class timings.

GWR/BR 1947+

The 'Kings' remained as the most powerful express motive power on the GWR and soon to be Western Region of British Railways. This is No. 6023 *King Edward II* at Iver. One of the three of the class that survive, it is preserved at Didcot, where it has been rebuilt to single-chimney form as it still was on this occasion.

The 'Castles' were the largest class of GWR express passenger locos and would remain in front-line service until replaced by diesels. The identity of this example is unclear.

Heading towards London, another of the class, No. 5070 *Sir Daniel Gooch*. Although these are GWR-built members of the class, further examples Nos. 7008–37 would be built under BR management between 1948 and 1950.

At the same location is one of the 'Grange' class of 4-6-0s, believed to be No. 6855 *Saighton Grange*.

The last GWR chief mechanical engineer, F.W. Hawksworth, introduced the 'County' class of 4-6-0s in 1945.Thirty were built, but the class was not perpetuated by BR, more 'Castles' being built instead. No. 1014 *County of Glamorgan* heads another London-bound express. It carries 'British Railways' lettering in Great Western style. Former GWR locomotives retained their pre-nationalisation numbers on cast plates.

The 'Hall' class continued as the main mixed traffic design. No. 6942 *Eshton Hall* heads a train of old wooden-bodied unfitted coal wagons.

Another unidentified 'Hall' on a passenger turn, again at Iver.

The Churchward 'Stars' and 'Saints' were coming to the end of their working lives and would all be withdrawn by 1958. 'Star' No. 403? finds employment on a parcels train.

Former GWR 'Star' class 4-6-0 No. 4035 *Queen Charlotte* works milk empties from London back to the West Country at Iver in 1948. This locomotive was built in 1910 and withdrawn in 1951. The train includes a number of demountable milk tanks with road wheels.

The 'Stars' could still find use on passenger workings though, and No. 401? seems to be making good progress through the cutting at Iver.

Mainstay of the suburban trains in the London area were the 61XX series of 2-6-2T locos. With express lamps set, this example heads down the main line.

A 43XX 2-6-0, No. 6300 at the head of a passenger train on the down local line.

By contrast, another 2-6-0 is routed on the main line with a fitted van train.

Brunel designed this handsome arch bridge to span the River Thames at Maidenhead. It remains the longest single-span brick arch in the world. The passenger train crossing it appears to be hauled by one of the nine Churchward 47XX 2-8-0s. This scene is from the 1950s as the first two coaches are BR built Mark 1s, probably in 'blood & custard' livery.

On the GW & GC route through High Wycombe, a 'Hall' heads a passenger train near Saunderton.

Another 'Hall' is working well on the climb through Saunderton.

The nature of the climb can be seen in this view of No. 5031 *Totnes Castle* near West Wycombe.

The 'King' class could also be found on this route working trains to Birmingham (Snow Hill).

In 1945, in an endeavour to combat the fuel crisis, a programme of converting selected locomotives to oil firing was started, it being considered that oil would be more economical than coal. Amongst the first to be converted were 10 GWR 28XX 2-8-0s that were renumbered in the 48XX series. The conversion programme was later abandoned and all GWR engines were converted back to coal by the end of 1948. One of the short-lived converted locos is seen here – the oil tank is clearly visible in the tender.

A WD 2-8-0 at the head of a train of coal wagons. The Westinghouse pump has been removed, but it looks from the cab side as though the old ROD number is still being carried.

Southern/BR at Hildenborough

Schools class 4-4-0 No. 30903 *Charterhouse* with its BR number painted on the buffer-beam.

No. 30928 *Stowe* however has a smoke-box door number plate. This is one of three of the class that survive in preservation.

Older 4-4-0 classes were still in front-line service. L1 class No. 31787 has a BR number on the buffer beam – although the tender still proclaims 'Southern'.

Another L1, this time with 'British Railways' spelled out in full on the tender side.

L class No. 1770. The D1, E1, L and L1 4-4-0 classes would last to the end of Kent coast steam in this area in 1962, and this was the last part of the country where 4-4-0s could regularly be seen on main line duties.

Still displaying full Southern identity is 'King Arthur' 4-6-0 No. 767 *Sir Valence*. 'King Arthurs' were the preferred power for the many relief boat trains.

Not present before the war were the Bulleid light Pacifics. Those allocated to the Kent Coast route were given names associated with the Battle of Britain, in recognition of the crucial role that the Kent airfields played in this campaign. No. 34077 in BR lettering on its Southern malachite green livery is yet to be named in this picture. It would later become *603 Squadron*.

Still in Southern Railway identity, No. 21C153 has already received the name *Sir Keith Park*.

Local trains would remain in the hands of the former SECR H class 0-4-4Ts until electrification. No. 31320 works a typical train of 'birdcage' stock on a Tonbridge–Redhill service.

A C class 0-6-0 works a hop-pickers' special train. During the harvesting season from late August–early September a large labour force of pickers was required, and hop-picking became a popular working holiday for Londoners. The main growing areas were along the Medway valley between Paddock Wood and Maidstone, and along the Hawkhurst branch. C class 0-6-0s and the 4-4-0 classes were used on the Hawkhurst trains because of the short shunting neck at the terminus.

Clapham Junction 1965

Main train of the day was the 'Bournemouth Belle' Pullman service, and on this occasion the down working has been entrusted to rebuilt 'West Country' No. 34021 *Dartmoor*.

Another down express is headed by No. 34042 *Dorchester*.

Heading for London is 'Merchant Navy' No. 35023 *Holland-Afrika Line*.

No. 34050 *Royal Observer Corps* draws empty stock into the sidings at Clapham Junction. Although all of these Pacifics are uncleaned, at least they still have their nameplates on. During the final year or so of service until electrification in 1967, many had their nameplates removed.

BR Standard 5 4-6-0 No. 73081 heads down the main line with a special van train for Southampton Docks. This had carried the name *Excalibur,* originally given to 'King Arthur' class 30736, but the nameplate appears to have been removed by this time. No. 73081 would be withdrawn in July 1966.

Passing through platform 6 on the Windsor side of the station, 73083 has charge of another train of covered vans, probably for Feltham yard.

Towards the end of steam on the Southern, empty coaching stock trains to and from Waterloo were worked by 2-6-2T or 2-6-4T types. BR class 3 2-6-2T No. 82033 brings a rake into the sidings that separate the Woking and Windsor lines. Under the grime, the loco is in lined BR green livery, having previously been allocated to the Western Region where anything that hauled passenger trains tended to get painted green.

The door handle just visible on the left of the picture reveals that it is the stock for the down 'Bournemouth Belle' that No. 82023 is about to take to Waterloo. This locomotive is in BR lined black livery.

No. 82033 again, this time tripping some mineral wagons towards Feltham yard. Despite lasting until the end of Southern steam, none of this class made it into preservation. A group are creating a 'new-build' example at the Severn Valley Railway.

BR 2-6-4T, No. 80095, prepares to draw another rake of carriages to Waterloo.

ODDS & SODS

The Dreamland Miniature Railway at Margate in the 1930s. The engine is lettered DMR No. 2 and carries the name *Prince Edward of Wales* on the splashers. The locomotive is a 'Little Giant' 4-4-2 originally built for the Rhyl Miniature Railway in 1911 by Basset-Lowke and designed by Henry Greenly. It was sold to Margate in 1920 and remained at Dreamland until 1968, when it was sold.

Another seaside miniature railway at Clacton. From this angle the wheel arrangement cannot be identified. It looks as if this is a steam outline, rather than steam powered machine.

The Rye and Camber Railway

During September 1936, I took advantage of a half-day excursion to Rye, one of the former Cinque Ports. Having inspected and photographed the Church of St Mary the Virgin (built in 1340), the Landgate, harbour, Ypres Museum, the Mermaid Inn with its cobbled courtway and the windmill, I had two more exposures left on my film which I wanted to use up.

On passing through a street I noticed a courtyard in which was a sign 'Rye and Camber Railway'. This aroused my interest so I investigated. There in a rudimentary station was a narrow-gauge petrol locomotive and a pair of coaches. I purchased a ticket for the ride to Camber Sands.

The train departed and trundled its way there slowly with many jerks and a load of only about three passengers. On arrival I was assailed by local fishermen who tried to persuade me to purchase their freshly caught fish! I declined, pointing out that I was on a photographic trip, and it would be inconvenient (and smelly) carrying wrapped fish all the way back to London.

I finished my film photographing the train and returned to Rye on the equally empty return train. I was not to visit Rye again until after the war. I looked for the railway again on this occasion, but it had been closed down.

The Rye and Camber was opened in July 1895 by the Rye and Camber Tramways Company. The line, of three-foot gauge, initially ran a distance of two miles to Camber Golf Links from where a ferry linked to the village of Rye Harbour. A half-mile extension was opened to Camber Sands on 13 July 1908. The engineer for the line was Mr (later Lieutenant-Colonel) H.F. Stephens, later to be associated with several other light railways, most notably the Kent & East Sussex. Original stock was a pair of Bagnall 2-4-0s and two coaches but the petrol loco had taken over by the time of my visit. Traffic was always light, with winter services ceasing in 1925. The army requisitioned the railway during the Second World War, public services ending on 4 September 1940. Although the army returned the line after the war it was not considered worth reopening.

The Rye and Camber Railway train at Rye.

A closer view of the Rye and Camber Railway's petrol locomotive.

Southend pier retains the record of being the world's longest. An electric railway was provided from 1890 when the present iron pier replaced the original wooden structure. The original trains worked right through the Second World War, when, although the pier was closed to the public, the trains carried personnel and supplies to gun emplacements mounted on it. Four new trains built by A.C. Cars of Thames Ditton were supplied in 1949. These would last until 1978 when the railway closed due to deterioration of the pier and the cost of repairs. Two new diesel trains re-opened a simplified railway in 1986.

Industrial Interlude

Memories of Sirapite

I was very pleased to read in *Old Glory* magazine of the £50,000 Heritage Lottery Fund award given to the Long Shop Museum at Leiston for the restoration of the Aveling & Porter geared locomotive *Sirapite* to working order. I have been following this story since it was first announced that the locomotive had surfaced with Preston Services in Kent. It was then acquired by the museum, which is located at the site where *Sirapite* spent most of its working life.

The Second World War had come to an end, and I had finally been demobbed from six years of National Service in March 1946. I was now free to indulge once more in my favourite pre-war hobbies of railways, photography and visiting the countryside. I also had two new cameras, a Zeiss Ikonta and a second-hand Leica IIIA, bought with my gratuity money, so I was eager to try these out.

One place I visited with my new cameras in 1946 was Aldeburgh in Suffolk. This was at the end of a branch from Saxmundham on the Ipswich to Lowestoft line. There I photographed the lovely church and the Moot Hall. From here I travelled back up the branch to Leiston for some more pictures. I took the abbey, or at least the pile of ruins which was all that remained of it.

It was while I was waiting back on the station for the infrequent service back to Saxmundham that I heard a strange rattling and clanking noise, and along a private siding by the branch line came a strange looking 0-4-0T locomotive, looking more like a traction engine on rails than a conventional railway locomotive. I realised what it was, for I had seen a photo of one of these strange machines before, although this was the first time I had seen one 'in the flesh'. It was of course an Aveling & Porter geared locomotive, named *Sirapite*, and it belonged to Richard Garrett & Sons Ltd Engineering Works, whose works and sidings were close to the line.

The well-known Aveling & Porter geared locomotive *Sirapite*, which was the works shunter for the Richard Garrett & Sons Engineering works at Leiston, Suffolk. It was built for the Mountfield gypsum mines in Sussex, passing to Garrett's in 1929 and working until 1962, when it was replaced by a battery electric engine until the line closed in 1968. The name is derived from a type of plaster made from hydrated gypsum.

When it stopped, I introduced myself to the driver and his mate the shunter, explaining that I was down for the day from London and would be going back on the next train. "Lunnon," said the driver, "That's a long way to go. I've never been Lunnon." I told him that I was interested in his engine and could I take a couple of photos? "I like that, come down on the track and you can take a picture of me and my mate and our darling *Sirapite*."

This I then did, but while I was in the process of taking the photos, a very smart car pulled up in the station yard and two smartly dressed gentlemen alighted. One of them addressed me: "I have noticed what you are doing and am most interested. Could you let me have copies of the photos of *Sirapite* that you have just taken?"

"Of course I can," I replied, "I have to send copies to the driver and shunter, so I will send yours also. But to whom should I address them?" I suspected from their interest that these might be directors of the Garrett company.

"Oh yes," he answered, "Benjamin Britten and Peter Pears at Aldeburgh. They all know me there." I was astounded at this. It was of course none other than the famous composer and his tenor friend. They lived at Aldeburgh where they were instrumental in founding the annual music festival in 1948.

The photos were duly sent and later acknowledged by *Sirapite*'s driver and by Benjamin Britten, who was delighted with the photographs. Then some six months later, I received another letter. It was from the wife of the driver, now his widow, for he had sadly passed away. She was pleased that I had taken her husband's photo and said it would be a tribute to his memory.

Many years later this photograph was published in a magazine. I was amazed, when a few weeks later, I received a letter from the sons of the driver in the photograph of *Sirapite*. They had seen the photo and recognised it as the one I had sent years ago. They even still had the letter I had sent to their father back in 1946. I am sure that they will be delighted to hear that their father's old engine will soon once again steam on its home ground.

Rear nearside view of *Sirapite* showing the traction engine style flywheel. This loco was privately preserved by Sir William McAlpine after withdrawal, and after many years out of circulation it returned to Leiston as a star feature of the Long Shop Museum at part of the former works. Part of the original works railway has been reinstated, opening on 1 June 2019.

EARLY PRESERVATION

Bluebell Railway in the 1960s

The Bluebell Railway has the distinction of being the first standard gauge preserved railway. Having finally closed in March 1958, the line reopened on 7 August 1960 over the 4.5 miles from Sheffield Park to Horstead Keynes, just a year after the founding of the Bluebell Railway Preservation Society. In 1960 the railway carried some 15,000 passengers, running at weekends only until the end of October. This was a highly creditable effort, when you consider that there was limited public awareness of the line, there were very few visitor attractions on offer, and that steam railways were still very much part of the everyday scene rather a major tourist industry. The Beeching Axe was yet to fall!

The first locomotive obtained by the new railway was an ex-LB&SCR 'Terrier' 0-6-0T, which was repainted to original livery as No. 55 *Stepney*. This was purchased with two coaches for a total of £750. It was seen here with the set of four Metropolitan Railway coaches that had been used on the Chesham branch until electrification.

The Bluebell Railway was able to acquire a number of locomotives directly from BR as they were withdrawn. Amongst these was the last former North London Railway engine, an 0-6-0T latterly No. 58850, which had ended its days on the Cromford & High Peak Line. Restored as LNWR No. 2650 it stands here at Horstead Keynes with a train for Sheffield Park.

Another acquisition was one of the three surviving Adams 4-4-2T radial tanks that had been retained for working the Axminster–Lyme Regis branch until 1960. No. 488 (BR No. 30583) was the most interesting of the trio because it had been sold to the East Kent Railway (part of the Colonel Stephens empire) in 1919. It was bought back by the Southern Railway in 1946 to provide backup for the line as the other two remaining locomotives were needing maintenance. No. 488 was repainted in LSWR livery in 1962.

Also acquired was the last GWR 'Dukedog' 4-4-0, No. 9017. It is seen here at Sheffield Park in 'as acquired' BR condition. It had been purchased privately and placed on loan by its owner.

Another 'Terrier' in the livery of the Newhaven Harbour Company heads the 'Wealden Rambler' service at Horstead Keynes. Note the third rail in place on the left-hand track. This was for the BR electric service to Haywards Heath via Ardingly. This route had been the means by which some of the acquired locomotives were delivered, and also saw some through railtours in the early years. However, the line closed to passengers in 1963. In 1997 the Bluebell Railway purchased the trackbed as far as Ardingly to safeguard its future. The line onwards to Haywards Heath remains in use for freight traffic to an aggregates depot at Ardingly.

P class 0-6-0T No. 27 at Sheffield Park with a two-coach train including the LNWR observation saloon. Note the weeds! The footbridge had not been installed at this time.

Diminutive SECR P class 0-6-0T No. 27 at Horstead Keynes. Withdrawn as BR No. 31027, this came to the railway in 1961 as the line's third engine. After running for two years as *Primrose*, it was repainted in SECR livery in 1963.

Looking somewhat forlorn at this time, but since restored, is *Baxter* (or *Captain Baxter* as it had been named until 1947), an 1877 0-4-0T built by Fletcher Jennings. This arrived on the railway in 1960 after a working life at the Dorking Greystone Lime Works, Betchworth.

The Blue Circle is an Aveling & Porter geared 2-2-0WT locomotive, looking even more like a traction engine than *Sirapite* at Leiston. It was built in 1926 for the Holborough Cement Co. Ltd at Snodland, Kent. In 1964 it was restored and presented to the Bluebell Railway by Associated Portland Cement Manufacturers Ltd. It has since moved on and in 2018 was at the Rushden & Higham Ferrers line in Northamptonshire.

Museum of British Transport, Clapham

The Museum of British Transport owed its origins to a report of 1951: *The Preservation of Relics and Records: Report to the British Transport Commission.* The 1951 report recommended that the existing railway museum at York should be retained, and two others created, one in London and one in Edinburgh, with a third to be opened in Cardiff at a later date. These would not just be railway museums, but also cover a wider spectrum of road public transport and canal transport, i.e. the full remit of the British Transport Commission. After an initial proposed site at Nine Elms was rejected, the bus (and former tram) garage at Clapham, which had closed with the cuts following the bus strike of 1958, was chosen as the London site.

The museum opened in two stages, and the first, the small exhibits section, opened in the two-storey administration block on 29 March 1961. It was divided into six galleries, featuring models, paintings, maps, tickets, uniforms and other miscellanea. One gallery was entitled 'London on wheels'. In the rear yard, some of the pre-war buses saved by London Transport, of K, S and NS types were displayed at the time.

The main hall opened on 29 May 1963 with 35,000sq ft available for large exhibits. Outside the main entrance a full-size replica of Stephenson's *Rocket* greeted visitors, whilst inside there was a range of rail and road exhibits, including 15 railway locomotives. Admission in 1963 cost 2/6d (121/2p) for adults and 1/6d for children.

The Museum of British Transport was closed on 23 April 1973, in preparation for the removal of stock to York for the new National Railway Museum. This was opened by HRH The Duke of Edinburgh on 27 September 1975, 150 years after the opening of the Stockton & Darlington Railway.

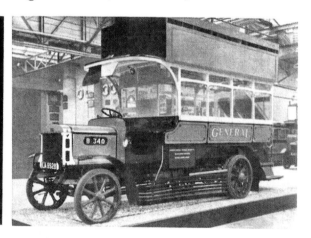

Museum of British Transport
Clapham High Street, London, SW4

Large Exhibits Section Opening 29 May 1963

Come ! See them at Clapham

Buses of yesteryear · Vintage road-vehicles
Historic locomotives · Railway coaches and wagons
Royal train suites

OPEN
10 am to 5.30 pm on weekdays

ADMISSION
Adults 2/6 Children 1/6 Special arrangements for School Parties

HOW TO GET THERE
UNDERGROUND : Northern Line to Clapham Common
BUSES : 35, 37, 45, 88, 118, 137, 155, 181, 189, to Clapham Common Station
GREEN LINE : 711, 712, 713
BRITISH RAILWAYS : Clapham, Clapham Junction or
Balham & Upper Tooting, then by bus

VISIT ALSO
The Railway Museum, York — exhibited are some of the
earliest locomotives in existence.
The Great Western Railway Museum, Swindon — here is
the thrilling story of the Great Western Railway.

It was probably inevitable that the world speed record holder A4 Pacific *Mallard* would be saved for the National Collection, and this was indeed the case. The loco was duly exhibited at Clapham. Less understandable though was the decision not to save *Flying Scotsman* for the Collection at the time. Luckily Alan Peglar stepped in and bought it privately.

Former Great Eastern Railway S56 class 0-6-0T No. 87. This became LNER class J69 No. 7087 and then 8633 on re-numbering. It was withdrawn as BR No. 68633.

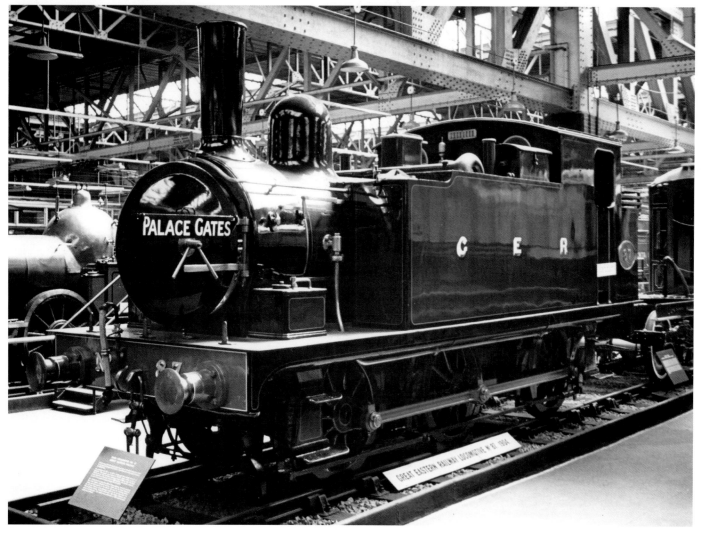

Former LB&SCR A1X 'Terrier' 0-6-0T *Boxhill*. Several others of this class survive on heritage railways.

Former LSWR Adams T3 4-4-0 No. 563. In 2017, this loco was 'de-selected' by the National Railway Museum and has passed to the Swanage Railway. In 2019 it was being restored to working order at the Flour Mill workshops in the Forest of Dean.

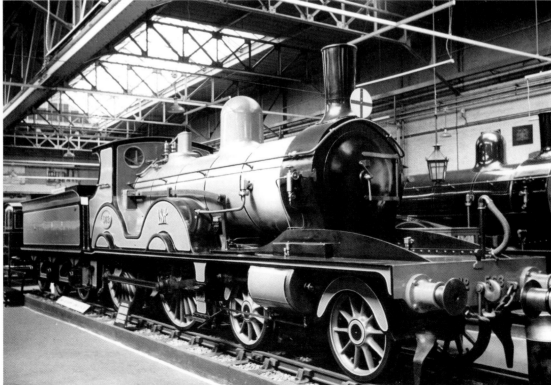

Furness Railway 0-4-0 No. 3 *Coppernob* dated back to 1846 and was the oldest loco on display at Clapham. This still had shrapnel holes in its firebox casing, sustained in a wartime bomb attack on Barrow-in-Furness station where it had formerly been displayed.

London & North Western Railway 2-2-2 No. 3020 *Cornwell* dates from a year later, being built at Crewe in 1847 to a Trevithick design. It was rebuilt by Ramsbottom in 1858. The driving wheels are of 8ft 6in diameter.

Metropolitan Railway Beyer Peacock 4-4-0T No. 23, built in 1866, survived by being used on the remote Brill branch until its closure in 1935. The loco was restored to original open-cab condition for display at Clapham. It can now be found at the London Transport Museum.

The ex-Wootton Tramway 1872 Aveling & Porter geared loco also passed to the London Transport Museum. However, this has now 'returned home' and is to be found at the Buckinghamshire Railway Centre at Quainton Road.

Opposite above: Former Lancashire & Yorkshire Railway 18in gauge locomotive *Wren* used to be employed at Horwich works. The trams visible behind this remind us that Clapham was not just a railway museum but also included buses, trolleybuses and trams (mostly from London).

Opposite below: Bulleid Pacific No. 34051 *Winston Churchill*, which hauled its namesake's funeral train, was also saved for the National Collection but was not displayed at Clapham due to lack of space. Instead the name and number plates were displayed.

'Exit through the gift shop' is the mantra of most modern museums, but the gift shop at Clapham was a more modest affair!

Invicta

Canterbury & Whitstable Railway 0-4-0 *Invicta*, built in 1829 by Robert Stephenson & Co. at Newcastle, is owned by the Transport Trust and on long-term loan to Canterbury City Council. For some seventy years it was plinthed in Dane John Gardens near the bus station. It was later moved to the Canterbury Heritage Museum until 2017. Following the closure of this site, the locomotive was moved to the Whitstable Community Museum & Gallery in June 2019.

Flying Scotsman

Photographing Flying Scotsman

Most photographers probably know the situation – you get a once-in-a-lifetime opportunity for a master shot, then something, or more likely somebody, goes and spoils the whole thing!

In 1968 I read that *Flying Scotsman* was to attempt to run non-stop from King's Cross to Edinburgh to celebrate the 40th anniversary of the first non-stop run it made in 1928. This was to take place on 1 May, 40 years to the day, and I was determined to record this event for posterity. This was something special – indeed it might be my last chance to photograph a steam train on the main line, as at that time the end of BR steam, then only remaining in the north-west, was nigh, and *Flying Scotsman* was the only locomotive that would then be allowed to run on the main line.

I carefully made my plan, choosing the location on Hadley Wood station where the train emerges from the north end of the tunnel. Rain or shine, I would be there on the morning anxiously waiting. The day started dull and cloudy, but I was prepared for this, having loaded my camera with a suitably fast film. I took a few shots while I waited. There was one of the short-lived, unsuccessful 'Baby Deltics' on an outer suburban train. Then came the unmistakeable full-throated roar of a 'Deltic' on the down 'Flying Scotsman' train, the successors on the service to the A3s and later A4s. This had departed the 'Cross' simultaneously with No. 4472 at 10.00am but had, of course, been allowed to run ahead.

There were a few other photographers beside me who had chosen the same location. We chatted amiably and exchanged reminiscences as we waited for the real event of the morning. Then came that familiar sound of the whistle and a moment later 4472 came bursting out of the tunnel mouth in all her glory, topping the 1 in 200 climb to Potters Bar, with Alan Peglar leaning out of the cab window and smiling.

I was concentrating on watching the viewfinder for the right moment to press the shutter, when all of a sudden we were distracted by some idiot who ran down the ramp right in front of us to take a picture. We shouted at him in no uncertain terms to get out of the way, but it

After the end of BR main line steam, a ban was put on all steam locomotives working over the national network. The only exception was the privately preserved *Flying Scotsman*, for which owner Alan Peglar had made a prior arrangement. A second tender had been purchased because of the removal of water troughs and columns. On 1 May 1968, shortly before the end of BR steam, No. 4472 bursts out of Hadley Wood tunnel on the day of its epic non-stop run to Edinburgh, 40 years to the day since the first non-stop run. The photograph is reproduced here as Reg adapted it at the time. (Reproduced here in black and white.)

was too late to do anything. The train was upon us and we just had to take it and hope for the best, or leave it.

The deed done, and despite having probably ruined our shots, he went away quite unapologetic, saying that he had just come off night shift and thought he would miss the event. For what it's worth I doubt if his 'mastershot' would have come out anyway as he only had a cheap Instamatic camera.

Disconsolate, I returned home and later developed the film. The negatives were fine, but there on my prize shot was the scruffy back view of our 'friend'. It could have been worse – at least it wasn't obscuring the train, but it was right in the foreground and couldn't be cropped out by making a selective enlargement. How, I thought, can I salvage this? Then a few weeks later I received a letter from a friend. He had sent me a brochure of the anniversary run, giving the mileage, gradient profiles etc. It was

printed in apple green and on the front in colour were the coats of arms of London and Edinburgh. I looked at this for a while and then inspiration struck. "Brilliant", I thought. "Just the right size". I made an enlargement of my picture, then carefully cut out the crests and mounted them over the offending interloper. Framed, and hanging on the wall, it looked quite appropriate and creative. No one would know that it was nearly a disaster. Of course, these days with a scanner and Photoshop it is possible to edit out such unwanted objects from a photograph, but that was not an option then.

The 1 May was also nearly a disaster for the 392.7 miles non-stop run. The story has been told before, how 4472 received a signal check at Tweedmouth and only just avoided coming to a standstill as she crawled over the Royal Border Bridge waiting for the lights to change. The return run was made successfully and again non-stop on May 4.

Rocket **Replica**

In 1979, the NRM's replica of Stephenson's *Rocket* was exhibited in steam on a length of track by the Albert Memorial in London's Hyde Park. This was in connection with the 150th anniversary of the Liverpool & Manchester Railway,

Didcot Railway Centre 1980s

The Didcot Railway Centre was founded by the Great Western Society, who took out a lease on the former Didcot engine shed in 1967, following its closure in 1965. Since then an impressive collection of locomotives, stock and artefacts have been amassed, displaying the history of the Great Western Railway.

There are few places that can match Didcot for authentic locoshed atmosphere. Inside the original running shed are 5900 *Hinderton Hall* and 'Modified Hall' 6998 *Burton Agnes Hall*.

Opposite: 2-6-0 No. 5327 stands by the coaling stage. On the Great Western Railway coal wagons were pushed up a ramp to the coaling tower. The coal was then unloaded into wheeled tubs which were manually tipped into the locomotive tenders.

First locomotive to arrive at Didcot was 14XX 2-4-0T No. 1466, seen approaching the Didcot Halt station on the demonstration line. On the right of the fence is the BR main line to Oxford for trains avoiding a station stop at Didcot.

The Great Western Society has not just collected locomotives, but also a full range of GWR carriages, wagons and artefacts. A selection of their finely restored wagons can be seen behind Churchward 1910 0-6-0ST No. 1363.

The last steam locomotive built for BR, *Evening Star*, had a woefully short working life of just four years. Retained for the National Collection, it has spent some time on loan to preserved railways, but most of its time in York Railway Museum. Here it is seen on a visit to Didcot Railway Centre in 1982. It makes light work of the demonstration line train.

The Great Western Railway pioneered the development of diesel railcars. Fortunately, three of these have been preserved, including No. 22 at Didcot, which is maintained in working order.

STEAM RETURNS TO LONDON: 1980s AND 1990s

For a while we had a railway museum almost on our doorsteps. The Grade II listed former North Woolwich station became a museum in 1984. It was formally opened by HM The Queen Mother on 20 November who arrived by train, hauled from Stratford by *Flying Scotsman*! In the old turntable pit was displayed ex. GER Y5 0-4-0ST No. 229. There were ambitious plans to run trains alongside the now singled line as far as Silvertown. This line closed in 2006, superseded by the parallel Docklands Light Railway, and in the run-up to the Olympics there were revived plans for a steam line. However, nothing happened – the museum was not in a

tourist area, and as it was run by Newham Council, it fell victim to spending cuts. The museum settled down to a static existence and gradual deterioration. By 2007 it was devoid of its dedicated curators and only open on certain Saturday and Sunday afternoons from 1–5pm.

2008 saw a further downturn in the museum's fortunes. The former GER 'Coffee Pot' Y5 0-4-0ST No. 229 was removed ahead of new building work starting alongside the station and returned to its owner's premises. Then many of the other exhibits were removed, several going to the East Anglian Railway Museum at Chappel & Wakes Colne. Finally in December the

Former Great Eastern Railway Y5 0-4-0ST No. 229 at the ill-fated North Woolwich Old Station Museum.

A 'Britannia' returns to Stratford! The doyen of the class was the star guest at an Open Day held at Stratford TMD on 9 July 1983. True to Stratford tradition the cab roof was given a coat of white paint for the occasion.

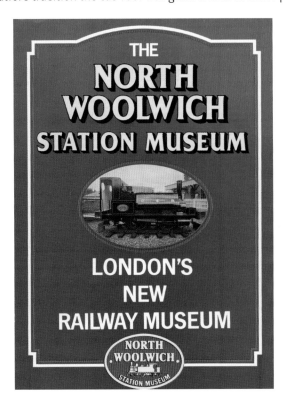

London Borough of Newham decided to close the museum. An officer's report to the council stated, 'It has not proved possible to find a partner to develop the museum into a visitor attraction and education venue.' In 2019 the station building was in a sorry state – boarded up and derelict.

Steam from Marylebone

Until 1985 there had been only occasional main line steam workings to or from London since *King George V* had run into Kensington Olympia in 1971 to end the steam ban placed in August 1968. The Post Office was planning a 'Famous Trains' stamp issue for January 1985 and wanted a loco in steam for the official launch. As *Sir Nigel Gresley* was the only locomotive depicted on the stamps to be preserved, this was chosen for the occasion. The line out of Marylebone had been proposed for closure, and running the train into

Marylebone was seen as something of a morale booster. No. 4498 arrived at Marylebone with the 'Thames-Avon Pullman' on 12 January. The Post Office launch was carried out on 21 January, after which tourists and visitors could ride to Lord's Tunnel and back behind No. 4498 for 50p.

After the success of this venture BR gave approval for a Sunday round trip to Stratford-upon-Avon to test the market. The first 'Thames-Avon Express' ran on 26 January and proved highly popular. This later became the 'Shakespeare Limited'. A range of different locomotives were brought in to work this and the various enthusiast charters that also ran over the route. Locomotives from all four pre-nationalisation companies had a chance to show their paces over the next three years, plus BR built 4-6-0 No. 75069. But the star of the show was undoubtedly the NRM's *Mallard* restored to running order and which worked three 'Shakespeare Limited' trains. However, all good things come to an end, and with engineering work possessions and resignalling of the Marylebone line, the steam workings finished at the end of 1988.

Former LMS Pacific No. 46229 *Duchess of Hamilton* is spare loco on this occasion and stands in Marylebone station with its support coach.

Opposite above: A 'Castle' back on its home ground. No. 7029 *Clun Castle* passes West Ruislip with a rail tour to Marylebone.

Opposite below: No. 4498 *Sir Nigel Gresley* heads a 'Thames-Avon Express' working in snowy conditions near Denham in January 1986.

Sir Nigel Gresley again, this time working 'The Cambridge Connection' on behalf of the Cambridge University Railway Club, seen at Denham in 1986. This photograph was also the subject of a painting by Jim Hayes.

LMS 'Black Five' No. 5305 now named *Alderman A. E. Draper* works the 'Risborough Venturer' railtour. This loco had been withdrawn from Lostock Hall depot in August 1968 and sent to Drapers of Hull for scrapping. However, the owner of the scrapyard, Alfred Draper, decided to preserve it and have it restored to running order. This was achieved in 1976. The 'Black Five' has been based on the Great Central Railway since 1996.

The National Railway Museum's 'King Arthur' No. 777 *Sir Lamiel* was another engine that was used on the Marylebone to Stratford-upon-Avon excursions, seen here near Seer Green.

Obviously Reg's favourite among the locomotives working from Marylebone was *Flying Scotsman*. Here it is storming along near Seer Green with 'The Shakespeare Limited' in June 1986.

Perhaps the biggest surprise though, was when A4 *Mallard* was extracted from display at the National Railway Museum, restored to working order and utilised on some of the Marylebone workings. Here the record breaker is caught near Denham.

Steam on the Met 1989–2000

As one door closes, another opens… Regular steam ended from Marylebone, but in 1989 it started on the Underground. To celebrate 100 years of the Chesham branch, steam trains ran between Chesham and Watford. These ran over the weekends of 1–2 and 8–9 July with steam haulage to Chesham and electric haulage with loco No. 12 *Sarah Siddons* on the return, there being no run-round facilities. A hired BR 4VEP EMU was used for stock. These trains proved so popular that in most of the following years 'Steam on the Met' steam trains were run between Amersham and Watford or Harrow-on-the Hill to Amersham. A variety of steam locomotives were brought in each year, along with a Class 20 diesel, and a set of carriages was acquired. These trains ran until 2000 when the division of London Underground Limited into separate infrastructure and operating companies was one reason cited for calling a stop to the annual event.

Steam locomotives featured in the first year, 1989, were Hawksworth 0-6-0PT No. 9466 and Metropolitan Railway 0-4-4T No. 1. The latter is seen entering Croxley on 1 July. This had been built at Neasden in 1898 as one of seven class E locomotives. It became L44 under London Transport ownership, where it continued in use on engineers' trains until 1963. After being bought for preservation it moved to Quainton Road (now the Buckinghamshire Railway Centre) in 1964. It was restored to steam in 1985 and since then has visited many heritage lines as well as working over the London Underground on many occasions. It has spent recent years until the end of 2019 based on the Epping Ongar Railway.

Also in use in 1989 and each year of operation thereafter was the 1922 electric locomotive No. 12 *Sarah Siddons*. There were originally 20 of these locomotives. They hauled trains from Aldgate to Rickmansworth, where BR steam locomotives took over onwards to Aylesbury. Withdrawn when electrification was extended to Amersham, No. 12 was retained originally for use as a brake block test locomotive. Here it is at the head of the train passing Croxley *en route* for Watford. Another of the class, No. 5 *John Hampden*, is preserved in the London Transport Museum.

The sole preserved N7 0-6-2T, No. 69621 double-heads with *Sarah Siddons* as it passes through Chorleywood in May 1992.

One of the two 57XX pannier tanks painted in London Transport livery is crossing the Grand Union Canal just after leaving Watford in 1993.

BR 2-6-4T No. 80079 enters Chorleywood, passing the disused but tastefully painted signal box. This locomotive featured in 1994 and 1995, while sister 80080 had featured in 1990.

The annual 'Steam on the Met' specials ceased after the 2000 season, although they were revived in 2013 for the 150 years of the Underground celebrations. Reg was particularly pleased to see one of the locomotives that featured in 2000 – the surviving GER B12 4-6-0 from the North Norfolk Railway. No. 61572 approaches Croxley on 27 May. When Reg first photographed the B12s at Liverpool Street and Stratford in the early 1930s he could hardly have imagined that he would still be photographing one of the class in steam nearly 70 years later!